CONTENTS

ONE QUESTION

It was a bright summer day in 2005, my mother had just brought us home from the optometrist who prescribed me my first pair of glasses. My eyesight was never terrible, but my nearsightedness did limit the extent of my vision as a child, unbeknownst to me. As soon as 10-year-old me got home that day, I remember walking directly over to the breakfast room windows overlooking my backyard. Glancing out with my new glasses on, I was utterly amazed at how the world looked from the inside of my house. The grass on the ground was clearer than I had ever seen before, the shed, the trees, and even the sky was clearer. I had always prior to this day seen a blurry world from that very same vantage point, a world where I simply accepted it to be that way without any understanding of the alternative view. But for me, putting on those glasses felt as if I had gained access to a new realm, it was almost frightening to me but a profoundly remarkable experience. "This is what you saw all along?" I rhetorically asked my mother. "What is your eyesight like?" I asked as I began to learn that other people viewed the world in very fundamentally different ways than I had. At that moment, my mindset had shifted to a new level, one that enabled me to contemplate more possibilities about the world around me than I could have before. The point of all of this is that after that day I had established an amplified curiosity and affinity for understanding how others see the world, and that would beautifully foreshadow many life events that followed.

Being part of a large family, I have two siblings and several cousins around the same age as me. As we grew with each other, I often found myself asking how they thought about the world. Each of us was very different in our own ways but clearly, I, out of all my family, seemed to be most deeply interested in science. I would casually notice that nobody in my circle really had the same level of deep curiosity as me. I *really* wanted to know how things worked, while the others, did not so much. Growing up in the late 1990s, Pokémon was one of the first hobbies I discovered. I was invested in knowing what each Pokémon was

like. I was able to remember their physical features, their powers, what kind or energy type, and what type of animal or plant they resembled in the real world. This passion for exploring the world carried into my teen years as I found myself drawn to The Science Channel and The Discovery Channel from 12 years old. Planet Earth, How the Universe Works with Michio Kaku, NOVA with Brian Greene, and Neil Degrasse Tyson, these shows were the staple of my scientific diet. I was deeply awed as I learned the way the Earth formed and what the stars were. Watching those popularizers of science explain the universe in ways a kid like me could understand only further fueled my curiosity. Before my parents came home from work, I would sit in front of the living room TV all by myself, indulge in that information, and build the foundation for my interest in real science which still lives inside of me today.

My brothers and I shared a 2003 Windows PC and I would make PowerPoint presentations, not just for school but for personal use, to simply express my thoughts in presentation form. Funnily enough, I recall making a PowerPoint about climate change in 2007 based on what I had learned from the Science Channel, shortly after the "Inconvenient Truth" came out. I distinctly remember the last slide which I captioned in big letters, "We're doomed." At the time my intention was that I was going to be showing these presentations to people, whether it be my brothers, my parents, or my friends that came over. Not only was I deeply interested in learning about the big ideas as a child, but I also had a passion for sharing them with other people, even if none were ever as interested as me. I didn't quite understand why nobody else cared as much about science as I hoped they would, although I didn't give it much thought until later down the road. Google Earth was also another tool that I would spend lots of time using, zooming in on the Grand Canyon and exploring the natural wonders of the world.

I would envision myself in those landscapes as there was something about going to places vastly unfamiliar to me that fascinated my being, and it still does. Expressing my creativity through invention was also something I loved to do. I remember when I had tried to make a bedroom light switch out of some yardsticks, tape, and wire hangers, which worked for about a day until it broke. I would draw designs and blueprints for new iPods or Gameboys with features that I wished to see. Creativity is deeply embedded in my DNA as it is in my brothers. Since my brothers and I were very close we did pretty much everything together and I am fond of those times. We would watch Nickelodeon's All That and other

TV shows, and we enjoyed reenacting the characters from those shows. We would memorize the lines and perform our own skits, and many skits we would invent on our own. Since I was good with electronics, I was known as the IT kid in my family. If anybody had an

issue with their computer or their phone, they would ask me to help and I would happily fix it. I enjoyed being the one they looked to for help and I was always encouraged by my family which is something I'm extremely grateful for today. They were very supportive of me which is one of the factors that made me who I am today. It is such an important thing to do for children, to make sure they understand their skills and talents are valuable and useful. The point of this chapter is to make you realize that my childhood was incredible and something I wouldn't trade for anything or have any other way, enriched with utterly precious and invaluable moments in my life. Far from the imagined darkened, deranged childhood that theists paint the average atheist as having.

I was baptized, took communion, and was confirmed in the Catholic Church. My parents had vaguely taught me about Christianity, the Biblical stories, and their major themes. Although my parents believed, they were liberal about our upbringing. They expected that I'd believe, but did not talk very much about it, as if it was some forbidden territory. So naturally, I treated it as such, as almost everybody I interacted with as a child did the same. We went to church fairly regularly, and I was a part of the Confraternity of Christian Doctrine (CCD) but would not take it very seriously. However, I believed in the god of the bible sincerely and took that seriously. It felt comfortable. I prayed sometimes, and when I did I truly thought I was talking to some kind of personal being that understood me and could read my mind. Since I was indoctrinated into the church as a child, I simply presumed it was universally standard to believe in "god" and it wouldn't even cross my mind that there were people who *didn't* believe in god . It was part of my personality, lingering in the back corner of my mind. I knew the belief was there but I never dared to question it, and I didn't feel the need to, after all, it was what everyone else believed so it must've been correct, I thought. Religion was akin to confidently wiping the hands clean and saying, "All done, we have it figured out". It was what it was. I would go 15 years of my life without questioning Christianity in any significant way until I got my first personal laptop in late 2009.

This was a Dell Latitude, a laughably slow computer but good enough for me. The world's knowledge was now at my fingertips, I was free to roam the Internet and learn things I've always wondered about. How do stars work? How does life work? Human evolution? I would spend hours watching YouTube videos with Neil Degrasse Tyson and other scientists who conveyed their scientific perspective of the world which was ever eye-opening for me. It was like unlocking a world that was never really explained to me. Think about it, at 15 years old, my only exposure to science was from what I had learned in school, which was practically zero, and the Science Channel on TV where I had to wait for the shows to go on air. Having the ability to now fully control which information I was being exposed to, led to what was essentially the second major realization in my life.

As I delved deeper into science, my belief in god remained unchanged and unbothered. I felt that science was a vaguely separate realm from religion and that god was simply absolutely true regardless. I remember one day stumbling upon a Neil DeGrasse Tyson talk in which he discusses religion and presents it in a negative manner, or so I took it that way. I did not like it at all, in retrospect it really made me feel uncomfortable, so instinctively, I reacted in disapproval. It felt personal. This belief that I had held onto for so long and was so fundamental to me, was now being threatened by one person. Doesn't he know that *everyone* believes? Doesn't he know that he is just one person against billions of us believers? Maybe he is just angry at the world, I thought. It didn't even once cross my mind that he was right about what he said. It was as if my mind had entirely omitted the logic that was coming out of Neil's mouth, it was invisible to me. Treating my belief in god as this unquestionable and forbidden topic to speak of publicly for all of my life, prevented me from actually hearing what he had to say, and instead, I dismissed what he said as just plain old disrespect. This marks my first real encounter with an open non-believer, and although I was left intellectually unfazed by it, I was not left without a lesson. I even held a small grudge against Neil Tyson because of his open agnosticism and harsh critiques of christianity, and mostly ignored any other religious videos of his for a few more years.

When I first stumbled upon the YouTube video "A Glorious Dawn" by Melodysheep in 2010, I was introduced to astronomer Carl Sagan who elegantly explained the science in a way that was borderline poetic. Science is really the embracing of the amazing universe we live in, and understanding how the cosmos works can be extremely moving. This is when I really became invested in learning more about astronomy and I eventually took astronomy courses in college because of Sagan. His Cosmos TV series became an important source of inspiration to continue science education. Unfortunately, I haven't taken away much from my 13 years in the public education system, as it was rather lackluster, but if there was one defining moment it would be during my last year of high school. I took an elective engineering course and my professor had an extensive background in research. He taught chemistry as well as many science courses in our school. Dr. Pangalos was his name, I will never forget it. He would wear a lab coat every day to school no matter the occasion, which at the time I thought was quirky seeing him in the halls but now I realize was badass. On the first day of Intro to Engineering class, he took us on a trip; not to anywhere fancy, but to the hallway where we followed him to a large window overlooking a field outside. He asked us one question and mind you, there were only a few students in the class, maybe fifteen. "What do you see out there?" he elegantly asked, as we looked at each other with confused faces. One student blurted out, "Well I see a soccer net, grass, and trees." With a smirk, Dr. P turned his head at us and said "Is that all"? There was a short pause that followed as we kept looking out the window. "Resources," he bluntly said, "Everything around you is a resource that can be utilized." He was making a point; engineering is about finding innovative new ways to use the basic things at your disposal. That is the ultimate goal of science and engineering, to progress society forward and benefit humanity. No teacher before him has ever really explained this to me, we've been subliminally taught that science is about memorizing facts. That is not what science is about, it is not just a body of knowledge. Science is a way of thinking, skeptically interrogating things; poking the universe. It took me until that class to recognize it.

In late 2014 while in college studying Geoscience, I took a job at UPS moving packages to pay for classes. At this point, I would consider myself scientifically proficient, I had done enough research and studying that the scientific method was fairly familiar to me. I still held the belief in god at this time, and that had been left unchanged throughout high school and into my early college years. At the UPS hub, I would move thousands of packages out of 50- foot long trailers onto a conveyor belt in the facility where they would be further re-distributed. One to two people in a trailer moved packages at a time and employees were assigned work based on how many packages were packed into the trailers. Heavier-packed trailers would get two people and vice versa. Since we would work for about an hour per trailer removing packages, we were paired with a partner for that long. We would strike up conversations which made the day go by faster. I made friends with one of the workers there named Bradley. He was a delightful person, middle-aged, from Jamaica, and even had a Jamaican accent which I enjoyed. He was known for being witty, always giving others life advice and cheering them up. Bradley was a devout christian and at the time I called myself a christian as well. We frequently talked whenever we were paired in a trailer because he was insightful and I admired that. Since he knew I had an interest in science and that I knew a bit, we would have frequent conversations about evolution, space, the big bang, etc. One April afternoon in 2015, we got into a discussion about religion. I was explaining to Bradley how humans are apes, and that we evolved from a chimpanzee-like ancestor. Bradley countered by saying that humans come from Adam and Eve according to the bible. He then asked me if I believed in the biblical story of Adam and Eve or evolution. In response, I attempted to agree with his point by saying I can believe in both at the same time. "Evolution *and* Adam and Eve can simultaneously be true", I casually muttered. Bradley stopped for a second, looked at me, and said "Mike, they can't both be right, it's either evolution or Adam and Eve." And at that moment, as much as I wanted to say that he was wrong, I thought about it. For the first time in my life, I actually took time to critically think about what I fundamentally believed. I stood there outside the trailer at a loss for words, I didn't have an answer for him that day. He gave me a pew bible to take home. I took it and threw it in the back of my car on the way home (I'm sorry Bradley if you're reading this.) But that night, I did as much research as I could, reading into the biblical stories and diving deeper into biology. The more I researched the more it reinforced that fact of evolution being true and the story of Adam and Eve being false. The facts and evidence overpowered the biblical story enough for me to cast doubt on the integrity of the bible. This quickly led to me casting doubt on the "god" concept entirely. But I still did not call myself an atheist. It took a few more days for me to finally concede to myself that I was at least agnostic on the matter. I was scared, I was uncomfortable, and I felt like I was stung by a bee. I was really stung by countering information and all it took was one question. Over the next few months, I gradually called myself an atheist, I felt I couldn't let my religion go. The fear of hell was still imprinted in my mind, leftover emotional baggage from 20 years of religious dogma and social pressures. It took me another few years for my fear of hell to slowly diminish.

Over the next few years, I temporarily delved into new-age "spirituality". Even though the indoctrination of religion had slowly waned, I still had this underlying desire to find something else. There has got to be something more out there, right? What if? These questions linger in our minds like dolphins swimming beneath the surface of the ocean, playfully popping back up every now and then to remind us of their presence. Some part of our brain relentlessly fights to believe that we have it all figured out in hopes of feeling comfortable and emotionally satisfied. If mere ancient religious myth doesn't have the answers, as it can not, then I thought perhaps there's something deeper I'm missing, something that science alone can not reach. How do we explain all of the ghost sightings that people claim to witness, heck, I have witnessed some strange things myself throughout my life that I couldn't explain. How about the ones who claim to see the afterlife? Why was I routinely seeing 11:11 and 3:33 on my phone? I had gradually become loosely sold on the idea of the Law of Attraction which states we attract what we think, and that reality is a reflection of our thoughts. I read more about Alan Watts, and Abraham Hicks and watched the movie called "The Secret." Yes, that seemed really nice. How wonderful that we are again at the center of reality. Are humans really the ground zero of all of existence? The saddening concession that I was merely falling victim to confirmation bias settled in. Although I loosely held onto that idea for a year or two, I maintained a secular attitude thanks to the scientific mental footing I had built for myself all those years prior. It enabled me to recognize where my fault was, no matter how badly I wanted to believe it; I even may still want to believe it. It may seem emotionally appealing to cling to new-age spirituality and even perhaps emotionally fulfilling, but I eventually concluded it's better to be certain of our claims before we believe in them. Even though I spent little time toying with the idea of spirituality, another great lesson emerged from that endeavor, another tool in my toolbag that would act as a reminder to remain cautious with ideas to come in the future.

VEGANISM

During the early summer of 2018, I was looking for the refresh button to my life. I was in my last year of college, and I had saved enough money to quit my job and pay for classes. I was traveling, looking for new experiences, things I had always dreamt of doing. I was finally free, but I wanted to ensure that I was doing it sustainably. I felt unhealthy, sluggish, and mentally tired; but now that I was able to do anything and commit to it, I delved into studying health. I studied nutrition for months during the summer of 2018, reading many articles and books I could find. I was in for a major surprise. The amount of information related to physiology and health is staggeringly high. Decades worth of data from millions of people all around the world within thousands of cohort studies, it was as if I was stalled in the middle of a highway of information. I was simply looking to find what foods to eat to really boost my physical health. I noticed plant-based foods were consistently the top recommendations by doctors and nutritionists; i.e whole grains, fruits, and vegetables. Another consensus I discovered was that meat products were largely unhealthy, especially red meat and processed meats. At the time, my diet consisted mainly of eggs for breakfast with sausage, granola bars, yogurts, lunch meats, and then hotdogs or burgers for dinner; the standard American diet. I ate on the go and didn't care much about diet, I also didn't care for the animals who made up those meats. In fact, it didn't cross my mind much where my food was coming from. I even thought vegetarians were weak and skinny, that they were overreactive. And vegans? Psh, I had no idea what vegans were until my cousin became vegan maybe a year prior which I thought was a bit *extreme*. That all changed for me after I took the time to learn.

At first, I went vegetarian thinking it would only be temporary, means to an end. I believed it was simply a good way to detoxify, but that's all. I quit eating meat altogether in one day and focused on getting more whole plant foods into my diet in hopes of seeing positive changes in my overall health. However, my interest in nutrition was growing so I decided to continue digging deeper into the research to really find how to optimize my health. One night, I was studying how the agriculture system works, hoping to find the best sources of food. Then there it was; a link to a video on factory farming. My curiosity led me to click the link and see what this was all about. It displayed the inside of a factory farm, something I had never seen before. I saw several extremely depressed cows with mud on their faces and bodies, mud that looked months old. They were tightly packed in dark rooms waiting in line to be slaughtered. I observed those helpless cows get stunned in the head by a factory worker and then get thrown onto the slaughter rack upside down, some kicking their legs, still alive and conscious as their bodies were being sliced open. I do not remember watching more than maybe 10 or 15 seconds before I became deeply disgusted and shut off my iPad, and I mean the core of my being was utterly disturbed. After watching, I quickly ran to my dogs to hug them, my eyes were teary. I looked my dogs in the eyes as my mind played back the memories I have had with them throughout our lives, I was recollecting all of the reasons why I loved my dogs. I grew up with them since they were puppies, and at that time they were in their elder years. As I was staring into the yellow-brown glow of their innocent eyes, I realized that there is an entirely dynamic personality behind those eyes. A personality like any human I've known, and most certainly like any other animal, with thoughts and feelings of their own. The third and perhaps most powerful realization in my life is that much of the cruelty humans cause is needless.

That night I remember eating a feta cheese salad and regrettably thinking 'what the hell'. I'm consuming a piece of cheese that is contributing to cruelty. I thought a little harder about where my food *actually* came from this time around. What was once just a harmless tasty piece of cheese, became a symbol of intense harm and cruelty. The next day I called myself vegan, and I haven't intentionally consumed animal products since. That was it. That's all it took for me to completely change my behavior moving forward. I sometimes wonder if I had not maintained secular thinking, would I have ever become vegan? I think in a way, there are parallels between the undertaking of veganism and atheism. They both take enough of a secular mindset to engage with their respective opposition from others, but more importantly, it takes courage to change behavior. In the same way it took courage to become an atheist, it takes a large amount of courage to become vegan. With information and knowledge comes courage and confidence. It's like giving a presentation in class, you can tell the students who are more confident in their presentation are the ones who studied more about their topic. Having a background in science allowed the transition to veganism to come about easier since I had a keener understanding of how my actions were detrimentally affecting others around me. I also learned from the exit from religion in the past to not hold onto any one idea or concept too dearly, I became a more intellectually fluid person, able to navigate the rivers of evidence in a focused manner, whichever conclusion they led to. All of this is why I believe I have made such a rapid change in my life. It underscores the largest benefit of maintaining secularism and scientific literacy; efficiency. Science brings clarity and focus to our understanding in multiple facets, in the same way the child version of myself was putting on those glasses for the first time unveiling a sharper world.

After becoming vegan, a lot of friends and family would curiously ask me why I switched. I became vegan because I no longer wanted to support factory farming, or any kind of animal farming since learning how devastating those practices can be to the animals, as well as to the planet and our health. In response, I would get the occasional smirk or laugh, along with "We are supposed to eat meat," "But other animals eat animals," "Where do you get protein", or "But you drive a car!" I began to realize these questions are only being asked because of how misinformed or ill-informed others are. First of all, veganism is not a diet, veganism is solely an ethical stance against animal cruelty. It's a lifestyle that seeks to exclude, as much as possible and practicable, exploitation and cruelty of animals. Being vegan doesn't mean I nervously watch my feet in every step I take, in a frantic attempt to prevent myself from squashing an ant. It doesn't mean I am a perfect human being who never causes harm to animals, and it doesn't mean I care more about animals than people. It means that I keep in mind the animals when I make a choice; on every trip to the grocery store, or clothing store, I recognize that my purchase can make an impact on someone's life. The goal is to practically minimize the harmful impacts my choices can have on others, not eliminate them. I believe if we have the power to choose, we ought to make the most ethical choices especially when it is practical to do so. We don't have to eat or wear the animals, and buying a plant-based option instead is practical. The position of the Academy of Nutrition and Dietetics is that well-maintained vegan diets are sustainable and adequate for all forms of human life. Other animals may eat other animals for survival needs, but we humans do not, we have grocery stores, we have choices, and thus we have responsibility.

Why do our choices matter? We live in an economy of supply and demand. Every purchase you make at a store triggers a higher demand for that product to be replaced and put back on the shelf. A higher demand necessitates a higher supply of products to be manufactured. In the case of meat, it's not *just* meat in a package you are purchasing. That meat on your plate was once part of a living being's body; it is the flesh of a cow, pig, or chicken. That animal had to be killed and slaughtered in order for its body parts to get to your plate. Therefore, when you purchase meat, you not only pay for that animal to be killed, but you are also triggering more animals to be slaughtered and killed in order to keep up with your demand. Where do the animals come from? The wild, right? Wrong. 99% of all the meat people consume in the US is factory farmed. Think of how many animals need to be killed to keep up with the amount of meat Americans consume; about 23 million animals every day are killed, that's 266 killed every second. Around the world, the number is 200 million land animals killed per day. A factory farm is exactly what it sounds like, a factory in which animals are stored and exploited for their body parts in an assembly line fashion. These factory-farmed animals are treated like objects and commodities, not sentient beings. To fit all of the animals, they are confined into small spaces, cages, or crates. Think of how uncomfortable it would be, to be crammed into a cage with other animals, barely able to move or be yourself. They do not see sunlight or get to roam free outdoors, in fact, the vast majority of factory-farmed animals never see daylight or get to breathe fresh air in their lives, as they await their impending dooms. There are 250,000 of these factory farms across America, animals being enclosed within these bleak facilities, without any windows or visitors allowed. No indication, from a typical outside observer, as to what happens behind closed doors.

Chickens are some of the most abused animals on the planet. The modern chicken has been artificially selected and bred to grow so big and quickly, that their leg bones frequently break under their own body weight. These chickens are not helped, they are left debilitated on the floor, unable to move for the rest of their lives. Their organs also frequently fail, and they suffer from heart attacks as their organs can not keep up with their body growth fueled by growth hormone injections. Chickens are not covered by the United States Humane Slaughter Act which protects from "needless suffering." They are typically killed using electrical water baths or gas which stun the chicken before being killed. They are painfully hung upside down by their feet on a conveyor. They are carried to the water bath where their heads are dunked into electrified water, their throats being slit after exiting the bath. However, out of nervousness and fear for their lives, many chickens lift their heads before being dunked in the electrified water, and therefore many are slaughtered while still fully conscious. And there is no rule or regulation to stop this, the demand for chicken is just too exceedingly high in the US.

Factory-farmed cows are exploited on a massive scale in the US, with 9 million female cows per year being forcibly impregnated and forced to produce milk. The females are confined indoors and walked back and forth to their milking stations. They are attached to machines that extract milk intended for their calves who have been taken away from their mothers within an hour after their birth. The calves are fed milk replacers while humans consume the cow milk intended for these calves. As the young cows grow older, they are debranded, dehorned, and their tails are docked. Cows naturally can live up to 20 years, however, on dairy farms, a cow is slaughtered once she can no longer produce milk at 3 years old, soon being sold for cheap meat or leather products. Investigation at these farms exposes widespread neglect of baby cows at these farms, who freeze outdoors in minus 20-degree weather, calves are shown dying from scours and pneumonia, never given medical care. Cows are very maternal mammals, they have been shown to cry for days after their babies are taken from them, they can also develop depression and even go helplessly searching for their calves after we humans snatch their babies away from them.

130 million factory-farmed pigs are slaughtered each year in the US alone, with most being kept indoors inside concrete pens. They are kept in confined spaces, some farms housing up to 2,500 pigs in one building. That is only if they make it to the slaughterhouse, as 1 million pigs die each year alone, just from the horrors

of transport. They suffer from extreme temperatures, squeezed so tightly in the back of trucks that their stomachs pop out of their bottoms, forced to inhale ammonia fumes and diesel exhaust. The crates in the farms allow no space for the pigs to move or turn around, let alone care for their piglets. These spaces cause boredom and stress for these highly intelligent animals. Many bite their neighbors out of anxiety or fear in those harsh conditions. For this reason, farmers often cut piglets' tails and clip their teeth without painkillers. The sheer number of animals killed for humans makes it impossible for them to be given painless deaths. Because of improper stunning, many pigs are sadly alive when they reach the scalding tank, which is intended to soften their skin and remove their hair. The U.S. Department of Agriculture documented 14 humane-slaughter violations at one processing plant, where inspectors found pigs who were walking and squealing after being stunned as many as four times. The CO_2 gas stunning process can take as much as a minute to go into effect, pigs are herded into gas chambers where they are gassed for roughly 90 seconds. The pigs cling to the cold metal cage, still conscious for up to a minute squealing in agonizing pain. As the line speeds increase, the pig's exposure to the gas decreases, not long enough to knock them fully unconscious. If the chamber is too overloaded, the stuns are less effective as well. Many of these pigs are fully aware and alive as their lungs are burned from the inside out. And this is just a fraction of what happens in animal farms across the world to all types of animals.

Who cares? They're just pigs! Well, we *should* care who these animals are as there seems to be much more to them than we give them credit for. Pigs are considered the fifth most intelligent animal on the planet, more intelligent than dogs, they are capable of playing video games with even more focus than chimpanzees. Pigs can learn very quickly, in fact, they are better trained than dogs. Mother pigs sing to their young while nursing. Young piglets recognize their own names and run to their mother's voices, just as humans do. Pigs are very affectionate, they enjoy snuggling close to one another and prefer to sleep nose to nose. Pigs have excellent object-location memory if they find food in a specific spot, they remember where it is for next time. They also have a sophisticated sense of direction, able to find their way home from long distances away. Pigs have unique personalities and characteristics and are loving animals. Chickens are able to recognize over 100 individual faces, not only of their fellow chickens but also of humans. Hens begin communicating with their chicks before they even hatch. When the babies are still inside their shells, the mother hen clucks softly to them and they chirp back. Chickens pass down knowledge from generation to generation as humans do. Chickens can empathize with peers in danger, and use their previous experiences to inform decision-making.

I can go on and on with amazing facts that demonstrate these animals are not just objects, but that they are sentient individuals with personalities of their own, fears and thoughts, and compassion for others. These are the same exact reasons we give for caring for and morally considering dogs and cats. However, we live in a strange world in which people view farm animals as mere objects, meant to be eaten for our pleasure, while some animals like dogs and cats are seen as part of our family. Why is this? When I discuss veganism, it is directed to people who share similar moral values as me. If you believe animal abuse is morally acceptable, I will never be able to convince you to go vegan, just as nobody will be able to convince someone like Jeffery Dahmer that it's wrong to eat other people. However, most of us *say* that we hate animal abuse, evidence of this is that I can scroll on Facebook and see countless people calling their dogs 'family,' or being heartbroken when a dog or cat is kicked, abused, or lost. If I posted someone eating a dog, it seems logical to predict most people would be outraged by that. Most can empathize with the animals and recognize that at least some of them feel pain. Most of us say we love animals because they are adorable and companions to us. Clearly, most people *should* be able to agree that veganism is ethically correct. I even recently came across a video of a family that held a birthday party for their dog, to which several other dogs were invited. Those dogs had no idea what was happening, no concept of what a birthday meant, yet those people treated the dogs like family, with an abundance of kindness and consideration. I guarantee that a majority of those people still pay to slaughter pigs, cows, and chickens on a daily basis. Why is it that some animals are treated with love and given tremendous moral consideration, while some other animals who are just as sentient, are treated with zero moral consideration as if they are supposed to be treated like trash? I sometimes wonder if we had domesticated pigs the way we domesticated dogs, their roles reversed, dogs stuffed in factory farms, and pigs were given birthday parties; would we still think pigs were meant to be harvested and enslaved? I think not. I think people are basing their judgments culturally, mindlessly accepting these stereotypes based on what they are used to, which to me, is a poor reason to slaughter innocent sentient beings. Here in the United States, we spout that we love freedom and would do anything to protect it, yet we take away the freedom of billions of animals every year. This is the epitome of hypocrisy. To people who share my moral values, there shouldn't be any good reason to slaughter an animal that did not have to die, one that wanted to be free. Protein is found in all plants, vegans can get plenty. Some will say, "But meat tastes good." If you think about how long your meals last, most would say they last ten, maybe fifteen minutes. I value the life of a sentient individual vastly more than I value fifteen minutes of pleasuring my tastebuds. Besides, there are over 50,000 plant-based foods that are delicious alternatives to animal flesh. The fundamental problem is clear, most people are not exposed to what happens to these animals enough to grasp the issue; most remain disconnected from the harsh reality they are imposing on others. This underlying problem manifests in the words we use, with a prime example being "humane slaughter." How could it be considered *humane* to slaughter and kill a sentient individual who did not need to die? We rarely are taught in schools the agricultural process and never taught what happens to the animals. We are definitely not taught that the animals we kill are sentient and intelligent nor that they are compassionate individuals. For 24 years of my life, even I was foolish enough to completely overlook the idea of giving any moral consideration to the animals I consumed. I failed to make the connection because I wasn't informed. If more of us understood *who* was behind the meat on our plate if more of us did our due diligence and learned more about what happens behind the closed doors of factory farms, more of us would be vegan.

In late 2019, I discovered the app TikTok. At the time I had been uploading some videos to YouTube, which were not going very well. I uploaded a few videos on climate change and veganism, as well as the 2018 elections. I expected videos to reach 50 maybe 60 people, and so they did. I would receive maybe 1 comment, and it was typically an insult. One commenter called me "Pinocchio" and a "liar." This had become my first interaction with ad hominem attacks coming from the opposing side. Anyone who gets public attention will at first feel upset when they receive negative feedback from strangers. At least, if they care as much about the integrity of their position as I did. I'd eventually take some of those videos down, and essentially give up my hopes of growing on social media. Later that year in November, I heard about TikTok from somewhere online. I heard it was trending so I decided to quickly make an account and see what it was all about. At the time I downloaded the app, nobody in my family or even my social circle knew about the app, and if they did, they simply said they would never download such a pointless app. However, I wondered what the hype was all about. I was introduced to the "for you" page for the first time, and I would scroll through mostly music videos and teenagers dancing to popular songs. As much as I wanted to say my friends were right about it being pointless, I realized just how much attention these videos were getting. I mean I was scrolling through videos with thousands of likes and views; people just dancing to music was getting all of this attention. I decided to test the app with my very first video, a 20-second video of me simply talking about how 2019 was a messy year for me. I simply posted it and forgot about the app for a few hours. Later on, I went back and noticed my video received over 500 views. I was astonished at how many views I got, especially because I quite literally had zero followers at the time. I thought to myself, that same video would've gotten zero views on YouTube. At that moment, I realized the potential TikTok had as a vehicle to gain traction on social media. I made more videos on politics, science, and then veganism, really looking to follow the current trends and merge education with entertainment. It was working, and after a few months I had accumulated 1000 followers and I felt accomplished. I was getting bits of my message out there, and people were liking it. Through the end of the year, I focused on making interesting, attention-grabbing videos, which rendered my channel gaining hundreds of thousands of followers and millions of video views. I was also networking with people in the same niche as me, meeting some great people as the TikTok algorithm was doing all the work. For the first time in my life, I finally saw that my years of education and feeling isolated in my thirst for knowledge were worth it.

As I was gaining social media attention, so was TikTok. What was once our private niche of secular creators had quickly become this expansive landscape of creators from all parts of the world, with all sorts of backgrounds. The religious/spiritual community was increasingly flocking to TikTok, trying to spread their pseudoscience and preaching. Naturally, as they reacted to my videos in defense of their religious ideology, I happily responded to their reactions. Debating became almost a hobby for me, as the quick thinking that it demanded improved my logic and communication skills. Whenever I would get stumped or lost as to which way to explain something to my opponent, I challenged myself to revise the way I would explain it. As the opposing fallacious points became repetitive, it allowed me to revise the route I would use to dissect their belief and undermine it, and this training rendered me a more effective debater. In virtue of my confidence in my own thinking, I see debating as a win-win. I get to challenge myself to improve, and I get to expose the main message I have to the audience. The audience deserves to see that there is indeed opposition to religious viewpoints and lots of it; especially when the topic of debate or discussion is as fundamental as the belief in "god." While the younger version of me wasn't aware of countering viewpoints about religion or eating animals, the present version of me wants to make *everyone* aware of the countering points because they can be deeply empowering. In retrospect, one question was all it took to profoundly change the way I saw the world around me; one question could have emerged in my younger mind that would have put me on a trajectory to becoming secular sooner. In my view, it is a tragedy that these discussions and debates are not as frequent as they are, and instead are still largely seen as taboo.

ARGUMENTS FOR GOD

The most common argument I've gotten for "god" is the argument from design. At first, this may seem like a compelling argument because it is deeply intuitive to us that things are made with agency. Watches, cars, buildings, and houses have builders or designers behind them, so it seems intuitive to conclude that the human body, with all of its complexity, must have required its own builder. However, does the sheer *complexity* of something indicate that it ought to have a designer or conscious intent behind it? Well, if we want to answer the question of whether or not we were designed by "god", then the proper step to take is to ask what human bodies are made of and how those came to be. The stuff of life consists of largely organic matter such as nucleic acids, amino acids, proteins, and phospholipids. These are organic molecules that biologists have a very good understanding of, some have even been made from scratch in labs such as the

Miller-Urey experiment; out of basic gasses found in the early Earth's atmosphere. Planetary biologists and geologists have detected most of these organic molecules in outer space, lying in the crevices of space rocks on other planets, meteorites, and even spewing from the plumes of underwater hydrothermal vents on the icy moons of Jupiter and Saturn. We know they are easily manufactured in the high temperature and high-pressure conditions of interstellar nebula clouds. These ingredients of life are so easily made by nature, they are bound to be extremely common throughout our galaxy, perhaps even our entire universe, seeding countless star systems. So, we have a good understanding of where the stuff of life comes from, the only question that remains is what explains how complex we are. I mean, how can these mere chemical molecules come together to form cells or eyes, or better yet the intricate complexity of the human brain? This is a question that has been asked for thousands of years, and for as long as we have been human, we haven't had an acceptable answer. That is until biological natural selection was discovered. The mechanism of biological evolution is natural selection. Life is a chemical system, building upon and restructuring itself over time; this is just what carbon molecule chains do. The bonding and reactive properties of carbon, allow it to be one of the sturdiest backbones of life. So, how does this explain the complexity of life? Small changes add up over time, and in retrospect are seen as bigger changes. For example, let's say an alien came to Earth and had no understanding of human development at all. The alien is fascinated by the complexity of the human body, it asks me how it works. I show the alien pictures of myself as a baby, then as a toddler, then as a teenager. Suddenly the alien becomes utterly confused. How, it asks, can that baby become a grown adult? I then explain to the alien how the change is constant, just incremental. Time has elapsed between when those snapshots were taken, and years of small changes add up to become the current, more complex adult version of me.

If we take a look at a color gradient displaying several colors in a linear blend, we can see if one were asked to identify the first blue color, it would be impossible to point out. First, we have to consider all of the transitional colors

Color gradient

that precede and supersede the band of pixels you label blue. Since the changes in colors horizontally are so incremental from pixel to pixel, we can group a large band and label that species "blue" since they are so similar in color. But the band of colors just before the "blue" species are also nearly identical. It's only in retrospect, looking hundreds of bands of pixels back can you point out the significant changes in species.

The change in species of colors happens not on a pixel-to-pixel basis, but on a band-to-band basis and over many bands. In this regard, it makes little sense to talk about the first blue since it would be completely arbitrary. Likewise, talking about the "first individual human" makes little sense since each individual within a species lies on a spectrum, with the human before it being virtually indistinguishable from the succeeding generation. This analogy works for evolution, in that biological evolution is constantly occurring, it is just microscopically incremental. The life that we see in the modern world, comes with 3 billion years of evolutionary baggage. Small changes in the genetic makeup starting with any one species, can lead to more complex species over generations. Fossils are analogous to the snapshots I presented to the alien, they are snapshots of the species as it was in that segment of time. This is the mechanism of evolution, and this is what explains why life is relatively complex. As you can see, no matter the level of complexity of a given entity, if the mechanism is known, a conscious designer or builder is never required. The only thing required is biochemistry or the natural laws of the universe. No rational modern person would look at the rain falling from the sky and ask, *who is up in the clouds making the rain?* There is no sign of intention behind the falling of rain, likewise, there is no sign of intention or design behind the human body. The fact that we mere humans have to constantly fix the errors made by the human body, produce eyeglasses and surgeries, and perform gene therapy by going into and fixing the flaws of our

DNA, is to me good evidence against intelligent design.

The universe has physical constants that seem to be finely tuned in a way to allow for life, so who tuned them? The world is perfect, just a tiny change in the value of gravity and we wouldn't be able to exist, right? This argument seems appealing especially because we have a natural disposition to think life is special. It seems so difficult to reconcile with the fact that conscious beings can exist in this way, with the world around us being complex. However, we have to understand that we may be being a bit pretentious here. "Perfection" is a relative term, it is not used in any objective sense. So if one labels humans "perfect," they would need to establish a standard as to understanding the *way* in which we are perfect. Simply spouting "Look how perfect it all is," doesn't tell us anything of significance. If making the argument that it's tuned for life, how would one know that the universe was finely tuned just for *us* when just as easily the universe could be finely tuned for rocks, cancerous tumors, and black holes since they all also exist under the same complex, rare conditions as life does. How are you analyzing the objects around you to gauge whether or not the universe is finely tuned for them? What is the difference between a universe finely tuned for humans and a universe finely tuned for black holes? If it's sheer complexity that necessitates fine-tuning, well then it may be true that the most complex thing we know of in the universe is the human brain. However, the complexity of human physiology is explained via natural selection taking place over time. It's not that we were placed here, in a perfectly complex state from the get-go, but that we adapted *to* the Earth's conditions over time gradually increasing in complexity, as the fittest organisms per their environments survived. Humans have existed on Earth for a mere couple million years, which means for the minimum of 13.7 billion years that we know preceded our formation, the universe existed happily fine without us. So to say the universe is finely tuned for us seems laughably silly at the very least, especially when considering that no other part of the universe had to exist for us to be here. We also should not assume fine-tuning in the first place as the laws of nature could be naturally necessary to the universe, in other words, could not have been any other way, which seems logically plausible. Even if there is fine-tuning of the physical constants, to which even many secular experts can agree, we can always offer a naturalistic explanation. What is stopping the possibility that there isn't agency behind the universe and there is simply a quantum mechanical field or fluctuation responsible for naturally driving the constants to be the way they are? There could also be a multiverse that spits out universes all the time, and we may happen to be one bubble universe out of an infinite amount of other bubble universes. Under this hypothesis, it would be rendered inevitable that eventually, a universe like ours would emerge.

Perhaps the most damaging critique of the theistic version of the fine-tuning argument is that their argument can apply to their "god" of choice as well. Clearly, the theist is confining god to having specific properties, like for example omniscience, omnibenevolence, consciousness, and omnipotence. If their god was any bit less omnipotent, or omnibenevolent, it would no longer be "god," and it wouldn't have made a universe like ours; the universe would likely be different if god was a bit eviler for example. Perhaps if god was significantly different in its properties it would have never been able to make a universe at all. Therefore, who finely tuned god in such a way that god would be determined to make a universe? The argument is a double-edged sword for theists as it does not actually offer any explanatory power over a naturalistic explanation. Since, if their defense is that god has those properties in virtue of being necessary, without any agency having to assign them to god, then we can say the same for the universe. The universe with its physical properties does not need agency behind it at all, it can be a necessary existence as well. Furthermore, the theist is assuming that the physical constants of nature are separate isolated values. There is no physical requirement that states the laws of nature must be split into isolated values for gravity and light or space. Since the laws of nature are descriptive, there may be some underlying unifying law of nature that is able to mathematically merge all of the physical constants we currently know into one entity. For example, if you alter the value of gravity, perhaps the other values are simultaneously altered to counterbalance, allowing the universe to still foster life even if the universe *was* different. We have much to learn about the universe before we can assert that fine-tuning exists and is attributed to a "god". A god would also not be constrained by certain constants in order for humans to exist. If god is all-powerful and all-knowing, he surely would be able to allow humans to exist anywhere under any circumstances. What is stopping god from allowing humans to live on Pluto? Is god really limited to certain parameters? To me, if we lived in a universe that was finely tuned for life then that should make life much more common and easy. Instead, we live in a universe that is difficult for life considering 99.9% of all life that has ever existed on Earth is now extinct, with five mass extinctions preceding us. Survival is the exception, extinction is the rule. Even for humans, life is hard, 10% of our species does not have access to clean drinking water.   Millions of humans have genetic disorders that render them debilitated, and constantly in pain. Yet we claim to be the main show of the universe. To me, it appears as if we live in the universe we would expect to live in, if we were guided by arbitrary laws of nature, and not intentionally placed this way by a loving being.

How did everything begin? What was the starting point? The next commonly used argument by theists in my experience is the cosmological argument. Another intuition-based notion of time; if everything we know has a beginning point, then what began our world? There must be something or *somebody* before our universe that made it. Seems like a perfectly valid conclusion to make. After all, we all begin to exist when we are born, there is a beginning to the day when the Sun comes up, a beginning to the night when the stars come out, and a beginning to the month and year; therefore the one who begins the universe is "god." Well, let's take a little closer look at what we really mean when we refer to the beginning of something. In the case of birth, it's not that I suddenly popped into existence ex nihilo, from nothing, as an embryo or a fertilized egg. No, the material that made up that "first" cell that became me, was as far as we can see, *always* there. The nucleic acids, proteins, and lipids that made up those cells were manufactured by my parents. And we can trace back every molecule and atom in that cell within my parents, back to the air my father breathed in, or the water my mother drank, or the food my father ate. And we can trace those further back to the formation of our solar system and even further back to the infinitesimally small fraction of time just after the Big Bang. This is when believers typically shout, 'Aha! That's when we began, at the Big Bang!' Even still, not necessarily so. The Big Bang only refers to the rapid inflation of the *pre-existing* universe. We do not know of a space or time before the initial Big Bang, and there need not be, as many scientific models by Penrose and Hawking allow an infinite, eternal, or cyclic universe. In other words, what we call our universe could have always existed in some form. The laws of thermodynamics allow us to understand that matter or energy is never created, only conserved; it merely changes. A true "beginning" is actually *never* observed.

Nothing begins to exist, things only appear to change through time, while the total sum energy of every object, every atom of the universe remains the same, zero. Where we set the starting points on the timeline of the universe is entirely

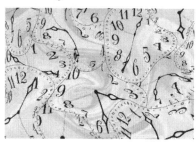

arbitrary. The beginning of the day at 12:00 am or at sunrise is not objectively empirical in the world, they are simply human-made markers made to divide and categorize the recognizable changes we observe into events. Think of a number line, with the number 0 placed at the center, stretching out to positive infinity, and also stretching out to negative infinity. We can arbitrarily set a beginning point at any point on the number line. We can place the Big Bang event at mark 0 or at mark 1 or at mark -1, but there is always a prior number. This is what we normally do when we talk about beginnings or endings, we are pointing to an arbitrary mark on the infinite number line of the universe.

The popular theistic counter to this is that if the universe was infinitely old into the past, there would have to traverse an infinite amount of time in order to get to the present moment; hence rendering an infinite past impossible. The problem with that counter is that it makes the assumption that time objectively passes, as the philosophical "A theory" of time posits. Einstein's relativity has challenged the notion of objective time, as time is demonstrably relative and the "B theory" of time is scientifically accurate. Time is a dimension of the universe, as are the three dimensions of space. Just as all of space exists out in the universe, so may all of time exist as the fourth dimension to our universe. What we call the past and future may all actually exist simultaneously according to Einstein. The illusion of the passage of time, this "persistent illusion" as Einstein called it, it may be a product of the brain or emerge from our conscious experience. There is no such universal clock of reality, ticking for everyone at the same time. In fact, relative to your velocity or gravity, no two clocks will ever agree. This is called time dilation. It turns out, your coordinates within the universe, your velocity, and even your mass can affect how "slow or fast" time seems to elapse for an observer. Time stops elapsing at the speed of light. Let me repeat, time stops elapsing at the speed of light. Imagine yourself on a clear night looking at the stars. A photon of light emitted from the core of that star, traveling to your eyeball, does not experience time nor distance from its perspective. From the perspective of the photon itself, as soon as it is emitted, it instantaneously reaches your eyeball. Relativity has drastically changed the way we see time itself. The point is time does not necessarily pass from moment to moment as it intuitively appears, so attempting to split time into an infinite number of fragments in order to make this counterargument to an infinite universe fails. The universe would not have to traverse infinite time to get to this moment, as time does not necessarily traverse. Making the error of stating 'time cannot be infinite' is making the same error as stating space cannot be infinite. Stephen Hawking is famous for using the analogy of nothing being north of the north pole. Perhaps asking where the beginning of the universe is, is akin to asking what is 'north of the North pole'. It is a malformed question as there is no such thing. The surface of the Earth has no starting or ending point, just as the universe which may take shape in various four-dimensional ways may have no starting or ending point.

Although the question of a 'beginning' may be the wrong question to ask, the question does a perfect job of getting us thinking about time itself. It is always fascinating to me to recall how mysterious time is to physicists. Time is perhaps the most obvious thing about our conscious existence, the thing we constantly encounter and battle with, the thing a handful throughout human history have really ever questioned in virtue of its familiarity. Yet, what exactly time is, is objectively unknown. Many physicists share the view that reality is truly eternal, and unchanging. Quantum theory allows us to describe the universe as one eternal unchanging quantum state, which holds the superposition of all possible quantum wave functions of the universe. So the supposed transition between different states of the universe may be nothing but an emergent experience of entanglement. In any case, common sense notions of time and space no longer help in modern science as they may have once done for the ancient philosophers of the past who invented the same arguments many theists are now attempting to use.

The last pillar of proclaimed 'evidence for god' theists propose is objective morality. Who decides what is right and wrong? There must be some cosmic judge whose job it is to oversee our actions and punish those who have done wrong and reward those who do good. Theists say there must be an objectively correct way to live and an objectively wrong way to live. And to that, I ask, why? Why *must* there be objectivity at all when it comes to morality? The idea that we can not achieve a sense of morality on our own without a magic cosmic judge is, to me, naive. Intuitively it may be appealing to cling to this false sense of objectivity because behaviors such as stealing and murder seem obviously wrong. And they are obviously wrong to the vast majority of us, but that doesn't necessarily mean they are *objectively* wrong. We act as if these actions are objectively wrong, but ultimately we are expressing our opinions when we lay out our moral map. And the funny thing is, so are the theists! They only *pretend* they have found access to objective moral truth as it aligns better with their personal narrative, but in reality, they are also subjectively expressing their opinion that "god" grounds morality. How do theists *know* that their Christian, Hindu, Islamic, or Judaic moral values are objective? Objectivity means a given proposition is true, independent of minds or stances. In order for morality to be objective, like gravity is objective, there would have to be some testable way of verifying that. But everything we claim to know about morality comes from our minds, it is never objectively verifiable. Morality is evidently rooted not in "god," but in brains. Humans, like many other mammals, have largely evolved to care for one another. We evolved the limbic system portion of our brains which processes emotions and empathy. This tool aided our survival as tribal animals, eventually leading to our species establishing strong social communities. This is why morality appears to be intuitive for us; it is deeply ingrained in our DNA. This is also why brain lesions or tumors can cause people to act more aggressively or lose empathy and commit violent acts they would have otherwise never considered before developing the disease. Morality is derived from empathy for others, as well as considering the consequences of our actions. This formula gives us what we need to obtain morality, a sense of what others would want if I were in their shoes. The conclusions we make with our emotional and logical brains, however, do not always equate to objectivity. The simple proposition "stealing is bad" is obviously intuitive to our emotional human brains, but not objectively true. I hold the anti-realist position that there is no law of the universe that states "stealing is bad." That is not to say that the contrary is an impossibility. It could very well be that there is such a law of the universe, however, I simply am not convinced of any such law. Simply proclaiming "god" grounds morality, does not help either.

The problem of evil is perhaps one of the greatest defeaters to a theistic "good god." Some theists may claim god is good, but how are they determining this? Is it simply the case that whatever god *says* is good in scripture is good? If so, then god's morality is merely its opinion, subject to change whenever god feels like it. Why then ought we follow god? It seems like claiming 'we ought to follow god's morality' is subjective in itself. Worse, god's morality can be exposed as barbaric, even to many christians, when we point to verses like Leviticus 20:13 or Deuteronomy 22:28. If christians agree that all of god's actions are good, yet god killed even innocent babies in the global flood, to which most christians would agree is bad, what does this say about their moral infrastructure? Christian morality is full of holes and contradictions if their god can do *anything* yet still be called good. Why does god allow childhood cancer? Why does there seem to be an extreme excess of unnecessary, gratuitous evil and suffering, evil beyond our control? A typical response to this would be that god always has a reason and every event that occurs is a part of god's greater plan. In that case, not only would anything god does be considered good, but anything that *people* do would be considered good. God allows that mass murderer to kill several people because he had a greater purpose for the victims as everything happens for a reason. Wouldn't this render genocide "good", because it was all a part of gods greater plan? This skeptical theist approach opens up Pandora's box.

Now, every event in the world occurs because it is fulfilling gods greater plan, his greater reason; every murder, every sexual assault, every stage four cancer diagnosis, every fatal car accident. If every event is good according to the theist, then they no longer have the ability to decipher between what is objectively good and what is objectively bad. They can no longer claim to know any action is objectively bad. Furthermore, the christian moral framework seems to be based on fear and loyalty, not good deeds. According to many denominations of christianity, repentance is the key to entering heaven. In this view, Hitler could have gone to heaven if he repented just before he died. Yet, someone like me, a generally good person who has never done anything remotely criminal, is going to be sent to hell in a handbasket, to be eternally tortured, simply because I did not repent. I did not believe it. Even if I had followed every godly law in the bible for my entire life, never "sinning", with the one exception that I did not believe; my fate would still be eternal hellfire. Is this justice; is this morality? Would a loving father allow their child to be tortured simply because their child rejected him? No sane person would call this a loving action, yet this is precisely the view that many theists hold. And it could all be solved by recognizing that morality doesn't come from a god, it comes from human minds. It's interesting to me that theists typically accuse atheists of stealing from their moral framework, yet it's actually the christians who typically steal from the secular moral framework when they make poor excuses for the atrocious laws and actions of their god.

These previous few counters are the main reasons why I think the theistic arguments fail. The bread and butter of theism is simply a conglomeration of philosophical nonsense meant to trick the gullible. Frankly, I think *all* theistic arguments fail. My main point here is that what people refer to when they say "god," is really indistinguishable from pure imagination. Not only is there no evidence for a "god" but the word "god" is ill-defined and means nothing of real significance. If I ask 100 believers what they think "god" is, I get 100 uniquely different answers. The norm is to just believe in something, and as we are typically taught 'there's gotta be something more out there.' But the elephant in the room remains, what do we mean by "god." The word is as useful as "blahdeedah." Most would use the word "higher power" or "supreme being" to describe god but what do *those* words really refer to? How can one say god is true, let alone that god is *possible* if nobody knows how those terms actually correlate to the real world? In science, we deal with very rigorous definitions, even in the most abstract theoretical sciences. We have to if we want to seriously take on reality and answer these big questions. Perhaps this is why I am interrogatively hard on theists because I am intellectually hard on myself with respect to what I believe, a product of my scientific upbringing. I am continuously putting my beliefs to the test. So to me, it is intellectually lazy and irresponsible to throw around the word "god" without anybody having any idea what it means. It only exacerbates the confusion that theism radiates, and distracts us from being critical and interrogative. Theists must do better if they want to be taken seriously by the rational, but they won't. They can't. Theism has zero explanatory power and makes zero novel testable predictions. Theism is not a theory, theism is not even able to achieve hypothesis status, as it's completely unfalsifiable even in concept. Theism is, at best, the assertion that "god" is behind everything. And it means nothing.

GOT EVIDENCE?

How do we know what we know? It is vastly more important, especially in modern times, to know *how* to get to the truth rather than simply knowing what the facts are. We are taught the facts in school, we have them regurgitated to us on a daily basis. The facts are even frequently taught to evolution deniers, climate change deniers, and young earth creationists. Yet, the facts go through one ear and out the other to many. Why is this? We don't emphasize enough to our students in classrooms *how* we know the things we know; how science actually works. We don't introduce nearly enough students to the beauty and elegance of science, the spiritually fulfilling uncovering of reality. Instead, we teach students that science is merely a collection of miscellaneous facts to be memorized and later tested on for how well they are memorized. If a teacher repeatedly tells their students the facts without ever ensuring they understand the method used to arrive at those conclusions, the students may eventually doubt the facts, and then gravitate towards beliefs that suit their intuitions or their preconceived conclusions. What's more disastrous, they will begin to devalue the tools and methods of science. This is precisely the underlying issue, many people today have no epistemic compass for which to navigate the world of information. We live in the information age. The average person today has access to virtually all of the knowledge and information the human species has ever discovered, at their fingertips. Yet tune into any social media network and it is littered with misinformation and pseudoscience. The flood of information has caused people to become increasingly reluctant to use their scientific compasses, and instead are trading them in for emotional compasses, searching for what feels good or what is entertaining. After all, science is hard, it seems. And it's easier to make arguments for my beliefs by appeasing the emotions of my friends who also possess emotional compasses. Decades of upholding this free-for-all mental framework, we foster a society that is trained to withhold from thorough investigation and trained to withhold from thinking critically about their beliefs. In a society digging a pseudo-intellectual hole for itself, the deeper the hole is dug, the more difficult it becomes to escape. The first solution is conversation. Although we live in the age of great misinformation, there is also a great silver lining to living in this time. For the first time in human history, as quickly as misinformation is spread, the countering facts can spread just as quickly. Much of education today is done online and people are increasingly able to be inspired to get educated online through discussion and inquiry. It's a level playing field, as everyone (ideally) has access to the same information and technology. It's a matter of people caring whether or not what they believe is accurate. How do we make people care about the accuracy of their beliefs in a world largely designed to reward the spread of pseudoscience and misinformation? I don't claim to have the answer to that challenge. However, I do see what helps.

People are not deliberately ignorant. Humans are a curious species. Children are born with a scientific mindset. They eagerly lift rocks to see what's underneath them, they repeatedly jump in puddles to see the water splash, and they bang pots and pans together to hear the noise they make. Children instinctively ask the big questions; 'why is the sky blue,' or 'why is the grass green.' This is the mindset of a scientist, and this is what science is! Science is all about poking the universe and seeing what happens. And humans do this naturally, it is how we investigate and discover things about reality. People already have the inner curiosity to know how things work. We must leverage that curiosity in order to show them the value of science. Instead, what school systems generally do is squander curiosity in children by flooding them with repetitive tests and quizzes that only assess how well a student can memorize a set of facts or equations. What this eventually trains the student is that science is merely an anxiety-inducing process that only leads to mindless facts that have been known for centuries. That's a tragic view of science. Instead, we should frequently allow students to use the tools and methods of science to make new discoveries on their own terms, this way they get a taste of what it's like to be at the frontier of understanding, to have a previous understanding of the world completely shattered and replaced with an entirely new and more refined understanding. Science *is* exceedingly rewarding, in fact, I'd argue vastly more spiritually rewarding and emotionally stimulating than any religion or superstition could dream of being. I can't think of any other human endeavor in which one can peel away at the layers of reality to reveal its deepest mysteries at the core and be sincerely awed. Nothing is as deeply exciting or satisfying, at least to me, as the moment when it clicks in my mind that I have scientifically understood a natural phenomenon that was once mysterious to me. It is what I love, it is what I live for, those moments. I am obsessed with knowledge, my inner flame of curiosity is burning hot and has never fizzled or smoked. I am just as curious now as I was as a child, and the reason being I had always grasped the ultimate goal of science; to gain a new powerful, and useful perspective on reality, that goes a step further from where we once were. If only more people could see science in that way, I think the world would be a much better place. I remember something I witnessed in college that deeply disappointed me. It occurred near the end of the semester and a couple of days after a test in a geochemistry course. It was one of the few days in which our professor gave us a very interesting lecture that had me, at least, very engaged. Yet one of the female students in front of me was visibly nervous the whole lecture, anxiously awaiting her test score. At the end of the lecture, our professor hands us our tests back and you could feel the energy of the room change as students braced for impact. The female student in front of me received her test and she slowly broke into tears. The classroom gradually noticed and students began to huddle around trying to comfort her. She was upset that her score was too low and she needed a higher grade to get into a certain program in the school. Several students then took the time to talk to her attempting to cheer her up. As I observed all of this taking place, I couldn't help but think about the absurdness of the situation. Instead of students being excited about the lecture and discussing science, the focus and attention were on a letter grade. How unfair of a circumstance; that was not how science deserves to be represented. We were taught something beautifully profound that day, but the school's grading system had a way of sucking the power and beauty out of science. Instead of being graded on how well they can memorize answers or fill in a multiple-choice quiz, students should be tested more frequently on the degree of impact that science has on their daily lives and their perspectives of the natural world. There is no clearer indicator of gaining scientific understanding than when it has altered your view of things, forcing you to stir up the courage to concede to that new, more enhanced, view.

The method of science is easy. Think very basically. If I want to know if there is a bee in a hive, I may poke it with a long stick and patiently observe. If I suddenly hear a high-pitched buzzing noise, something which we know is the typical sound of a large flying insect, I have one piece of evidence and a justified reason for my belief that there is a flying insect in that beehive. I repeat the test again by poking it another time to gain credence as to whether or not what I've heard is likely to be an insect. Then I may look at using a separate test, perhaps I attach a colorful flower to the end of the stick in hopes of attracting the potential bee, and so I patiently wait to see if there is a specific response again. If the first test is successful, I have just gained some evidence for the insect, if both tests are successful, I now have a justified belief in the bee. To use a more complex example, let's say I want to understand photosynthesis. I want to know what makes a plant grow, and in my observations of the world, I notice that plants grow less in shady areas versus plants in sunnier areas. I hypothesize that sunlight can affect a plant's growth, and I predict that if a plant gets little sun its growth will be less than optimal. I set up an experiment to test my hypothesis with two separate plants of the same species. I allow one to get 12 hours of sunlight per day for three weeks, while the other only gets 2 hours of sun per day for the same three weeks. All other variables are equal. I measured the changes in the growth of the plants, and the color of their leaves throughout the experiment. In the end, I analyzed the data and found that the plant which received more sunlight had more growth as well as darker healthier leaves. This is evidence that indicates sunlight plays a role in plant growth, and I can repeat this experiment with more sets of plants or with different sun exposure amounts to verify my results and to factor out any potential outliers. I can also have other people perform this experiment, all around the world, to check my results, and filter out any human error. We asked a question, made a prediction about an outcome, and tested this prediction multiple times. I can further experiment by changing other variables within this experiment like the amount of water used, air content, soil content, etc. This would allow me to get further insight into the growth of a plant. We use our senses and prior knowledge of the world, to pry deeper into the mechanisms of something that was once mysterious.

Science is a self-correcting method that builds and improves upon itself as we explore the world around us. The results we get in science are only as good as the evidence is. The more experiments we can do, the more variables we can test, and the more evidence (testable data) we obtain, the closer we get to understanding what's really happening around us, aka truth. You may be able to see now the reason spouting "You are the evidence of god!" is not actually evidence. It does not count as evidence because it is unable to be falsified, it has not been demonstrated that I indicate the existence of a "god". It is merely a claim. If I simply told you that DNA is evidence of evolution, you would have no reason to believe me. Until I showed you the genetic mutations and chromosome fusions and the molecular homology within DNA that indicates genetic changes, you would then understand it was evidence of evolution. Do not just assert "I am the evidence" of god, show me. How can one experiment with me in a way that would indicate I was "created" by god? Moving on, if we perform enough experiments and stir up enough facts that support a given explanation for some observable phenomena, then we have established a scientific theory. This means we have an explanation, backed by tons of evidence, that can make novel predictions about something we may observe in the future. If I can come up with an explanation that has the ability to reliably predict specific events in the future which come true when tested, that is a sign of a successful scientific theory. These are some of the most profound moments in science for scientists, highlights of an entire career when a prediction is made and is shown to be true. This also further solidifies a theory, for example, let's take the theory of evolution via natural selection. Evolution is a verifiable fact as it refers to observable genetic changes over time, and is explained by natural selection. Natural selection explains why we observe the fact of biological evolution. Charles Darwin, when developing the theory of evolution via natural selection, made several predictions that have since been shown to be true. For example, a species of insect he predicted existed would have a proboscis long enough to reach the nectar at the bottom of one flower; it was discovered four decades later in 1903 and called

Darwin's Hawk Moth. But even more amazing was an evolutionary prediction in 1999 made by paleontologist Neil Shubin. If evolution were true we should be able to find a transitional fossil between fish and land animals dating back 375 million years ago, signifying one of the first species of land animal. Shubin and his team looked at geological strata located in the Arctic, which contains layers dating back to those times. They were also located in an area where Shubin predicted this type of species would exist; near the equator. Plate tectonics has since shifted the current North American continent from its previous location at the equator. In 2004, the team discovered the transitional fossil Tiktaalik. This fossil contained fish-like scales and fins, as well as a crocodile-like flat head with its eyes on top. It also contained bone structure in its fins that corresponded to bones of land animals, indicating that this was the missing link Tiktaalik. Scientists now agree Tiktaalik was one of the first animals that ever walked on land. Moreover, many elements on the periodic table were predicted to exist by chemist Mendeleev such as Boron, Aluminum and Silicon only to be discovered years later; some even decades after Mendeleev's death. Another core example is Einstein and his general theory of relativity in which he predicts gravitational waves. Einstein theorized that if the fabric of space-time is elastic and can bend and fold like water on the surface of the ocean, we should be able to see gravity waves caused by the movements of mass in space. In 2016, one hundred years after Einstein's prediction, gravitational waves were finally detected and confirmed by scientists. Just think about that, with the physical equations discovered via science, Einstein was able to peer into this underlying truth about reality a hundred years before modern scientists, who had just obtained the capacity to perform the experiment sophisticated enough to confirm it. This is the predictive power of scientific theories.

The laws of nature are scientific descriptions of the mechanisms by which the world works. In science, it is not assumed that theories are the most fundamental explanations for the universe. In fact, scientists are continuously searching for better theories with more explanatory power. So although Einstein's theories work to explain a cross-section of reality, it does not explain everything about space-time or gravity. There is still digging to be done and scientists are never complacent with any one idea. Most theoretical physicists today are searching for a more unified theory that ties in relativity with quantum mechanics. Einstein avoided utilizing quantum mechanics in his theories, but today we know that was a mistake. Quantum mechanics we know now, is a vital part of understanding existence and it really pertains to the world we can't directly see; the quantum world. The point I want to get across is that science is not absolutely conclusive, ever. We only attempt in science to arrive at an approximate truth, in other words, the most convincing and evidence-based conclusions available at the time. Although science is the most powerful tool we have for unlocking the mysteries of reality, the laws of nature we use in science are merely descriptive. This might be dissatisfying to some, but it only highlights the power of the fruits of science. Recognize that even when a scientific theory or law is not fundamentally complete, it always has utility. Newton's law of gravitation is incomplete, in the sense that it doesn't consider a deeper understanding of the curvature of space-time. So although I would have a hard time predicting the orbits of planets with Newton's law of gravity, I can still use it to predict the velocity of an apple at any point in its fall to the ground, regardless of how accurate Newton's view of gravity is. So in that aspect, Newton's law of gravity will forever be correct, enshrined as law in science, as a mathematical description for the mechanisms of gravity. Even though the complete explanation of gravity itself is still unknown to humans.

Gravity is still unknown to humans. I mean, we know what we mean when we talk about gravity, but our understanding of it is still only surface-level. *Time* is still unknown to humans. Some of the most familiar and intuitive concepts to any human experience on a seamless and consistent basis, yet they are still some of the least understood. This is the ultimate lesson in science, it should remind us daily not just of how much that is known, but of how much that isn't known. Science mainly resides in the unknown. We live in a culture that prizes science to a large degree, everything we know and love about the modern world depends on it, and this may give off the illusion to the scientifically illiterate that it has all knowledge. Even the way I describe science may give the reader the impression that I hold to science like a religion. Science has led to so much success in our world that it is seen as an immediate go-to for those who are scientifically literate and an immediate no-go for those who are scientifically illiterate. It's far too easy to get lost in the controversy and conspiracy that we lose focus on the meaning of science. It's not here to tell us all of the answers like a crystal ball, nor is it here to say that anything outside of its domain cannot exist. Science is a compass, a way of navigating through the ocean of information we see the universe as. And like a compass, it can't tell you everything about your destination; it can only lead you there based on your understanding of the basic geographic principles, north, south, east, or west. And the beautiful thing is that there is no ultimate destination in science, we are simply sailing across the oceans, mesmerized by anything we find. What lies beyond the horizon, is always going to be unknown, until a better way of navigating the oceans is discovered. But until then, and that day may never come, embracing science is embracing the unknown, the mystery of it all. If you are shaking your head thinking ' *there's gotta be something more out there that science cannot see* '; that is a fantastic idea! I never want one to get the impression that science says there can't be something beyond the horizon of knowledge. The common widespread allegation of appealing to scientism on part of the believer is uncalled for. However, it's important that you provide a way or method that is able to achieve those answers. If you think there is a "god" and it is beyond science, then show us how you know that. Science would be the first one to attempt to find it or help find it if you could outline to the rest of us how you got there. After all, if you are honest and true in the pursuit of truth, you should care more about how you know than claiming to know.

CARL SAGAN'S LEGACY

To me, Carl Sagan is one of the most influential people the world has ever known. His relentless pursuit of truth, persistent skepticism, and elegant representation of science reflecting the emotional richness of the journey is, to say the least, exceedingly admirable. The most uplifting emotional experiences I have ever had in my life have been this way of loving nature as it really is, without projecting my fears or fantasies onto it, solely having a sense of deep gratitude for what is real. Carl Sagan brings us there like no other. Learning how stars work, the elements being produced in the cores of stars billions of years ago, that star stuff is what I am made of; it's a profound journey. Pondering the fact that we can trace back my origins to the violent death of a star, light years away and billions of years ago, makes me want to just tell the world. As Carl Sagan said, 'When you're in love, you want to tell the world.' He wanted to share his passion for science with the public, and to me, that is the legacy of his tenure on this planet. Carl Sagan understood that each of us is searching for our place in the universe, searching for purpose and belonging. The thrilling undertaking of science is the open exploration of cosmic wonders. Science quenches that thirst for an emotionally uplifting human experience that no other religion or spirituality can even come close to satisfying, because science isn't just awe-inspiring, science is real. Sagan was able to convey that message to us so elegantly throughout his life's work, and he had the courage to share it with the world. The best part is that his journey had a humble beginning. It started when Carl's parents brought him to the 1939 New York World's Fair when he was around 5 years old. Carl was captivated by the progressive theme called "The World of Tomorrow" which demonstrated a cleaner, more streamlined society where poverty was unheard of. Various upcoming technologies and visions of futuristic cities were displayed at the fair. This was his first encounter with the exciting possibilities that science and technology can enable. A couple of years later, Carl's mother took him to the New York public library where young Carl asked the librarian for a book about stars. The librarian came back and handed him a book of Hollywood stars. Few around him understood much about science, yet as a child, Carl was so eager to get answers to his questions. When he finally got a hold of the astronomy book, he read as much as he could in one sitting, trying to figure out what the stars were. He realized that if the stars are just other suns far away, perhaps there are other planets around those stars like Earth with people living on them. Carl delved into science fiction, where aliens

on Mars were typically the main characters of these narratives. Carl became so infatuated with these, unbeknownst to him, fictional characters that he sometimes found himself looking up at the sky wishing for the Martians to send him up to Mars. At the end of World War II, Carl heard about the V2 rockets that Germany used to bomb England. The idea of rockets fascinated him since he thought he may be able to use them to get to Mars and talk to the Martians. From that point, it became clear that Carl wanted to study astronomy. He went to high school in New Jersey and excelled there, as his teachers commonly noted, with astronomy still being his main interest. At the age of 16, he accepted a scholarship at the University of Chicago where Sagan went on to earn his M.S. degree in Physics and Ph.D. in astronomy and astrophysics. Carl's Ph.D. thesis predicted a greenhouse effect on Venus, which was a major breakthrough at the time, something which is typically unheard of for most Ph.D. candidates. Sagan was soon offered work at NASA where he helped design the Mariner 2 spacecraft, the first spacecraft to fly by Venus, let alone any planet. The spacecraft confirmed Sagan's idea that Venus was exceedingly hot in temperature at its surface. In 1976, the Viking I lander touched the surface of Mars and took several photos, for which Sagan helped plan and select landing sites. By 1977, Sagan quickly grew in popularity with appearances on the Tonight Show, several best-selling books, and was featured on the cover of widely popular magazines. Sagan next worked on the Voyager spacecraft where he produced a Golden Record to be sent along with the spacecraft to voyage the solar system and beyond, for billions of years. On the Voyager Golden Record are photos of Earth, people of Earth, music including Beethoven's 5th and The Beatles' Here Comes the Sun, sounds of nature, and directions on how to use the record in case an extraterrestrial species were to discover it at any point in the future. Carl also decided to add an EEG to the record, which is a recorded measurement of brainwaves. He thought the brainwaves which correlated to thoughts could potentially be deciphered by an intelligent alien in the future. Ann Druyan, whom Carl was dating, volunteered to provide the brain waves for the project. On June 1st, 1977, two days before her EEG was scheduled, Ann shared an important phone call with Carl, in which they decided to get married. Sagan and Ann Druyan had just fallen in love with each other while they were working on the record. And on June 3rd, 1977 her brain waves were recorded, echoes of that romantic moment reverberating through her mind, the brainwaves of someone who was euphorically in love.

Those recordings were included in the record, and present day, the spacecraft is just beyond the heliosphere, just beyond our solar system to voyage across the galaxy for millions of years.

"My feelings as a 27-year-old woman, madly fallen in love, they're on that record," says Druyan. "It's forever. It'll be true 100 million years from now. For me Voyager is a kind of joy so powerful, it robs you of your fear of death." - Ann Druyan

Cosmos was the next project that Carl and Ann worked on, a 13-part TV series on the history of astronomy and the exploration of space. It was released in September 1980, a year after Sagan's father died. Cosmos, which is still one of the most successful educational TV series ever, cemented Carl as one of the greatest scientific popularizers in American history. Cosmos was chillingly natural for Sagan and this was evident in watching the show. His knowledge and scientific literacy in almost every category of science were beyond anything I have seen anyone achieve. He took the audience on journeys to the micro world of our cells and DNA, to the planets and stars, and to the fundamental nature of space and time. The show is seeping with thrilling journeys and a clear sense that Carl was passionate about exploring the wonders of the cosmos and sharing this perspective with the world. His performance could easily engage any honest audience member and even inspire them to get into a STEM field, as it did for many. Carl understood that all of us are curious, and Cosmos is a wonderful tool to leverage that curiosity into becoming empowered people.

In the 1980s, Carl along with a few other scientists published a paper on the global consequences of a nuclear winter. This was at the height of the threats of nuclear war during the Cold War era. They found that if even a small nuclear war were to break out, the temperature of the planet would decrease by at least 15 to 25 degrees Celsius which would essentially necessitate a global extinction. Understanding what was at stake, Sagan took more time to delve into activism over this decade. In 1985 he testified before Congress on climate change, how the greenhouse effect is changing the global climate system and discussed potential solutions.

In 1990, Voyager 1 spacecraft was about 4 billion miles away from the Earth, and still just able to see the Earth as a small dot of light from that vantage point. As the spacecraft was exiting our local cosmic neighborhood near the planet Neptune, Sagan convinced NASA to take one last photo looking back toward Earth. The spacecraft captured the image below, where Earth appears as a tiny point of light, a mere fraction of a pixel, in front of a scattered sun ray, against a vast ocean of darkness and emptiness we call the universe. This is the cosmic perspective, a demonstration of our true place in the cosmos. From this vantage point, there is no sign of our position in the universe being somehow "perfect" or "special". This photo can change the way one sees their place in the universe forever. Sagan reflected on the image in his 1994 book "Pale Blue Dot" with this incredible excerpt:

"Look again at that dot. That's here. That's home. That's us. On it everyone you love, everyone you know, everyone you ever heard of, every human being who ever was, lived out their lives. The aggregate of our joy and suffering, thousands of confident religions, ideologies, and economic doctrines, every hunter and forager, every hero and coward, every creator and destroyer of civilization, every king and peasant, every young couple in love, every mother and father, hopeful child, inventor, and explorer, every teacher of morals, every corrupt politician, every "superstar," every "supreme leader," every saint and sinner in the history of our species lived there—on a mote of dust suspended in a sunbeam.

The Earth is a very small stage in a vast cosmic arena. Think of the rivers of blood spilled by all those generals and emperors so that, in glory and triumph, they could become the momentary masters of a fraction of a dot. Think of the endless cruelties visited by the inhabitants of one corner of this pixel on the scarcely distinguishable inhabitants of some other corner, how frequent their misunderstandings, how eager they are to kill one another, how fervent their hatreds.

Our posturings, our imagined self-importance, the

delusion that we have some privileged position in the Universe, are challenged by this point of pale light. Our planet is a lonely speck in the great enveloping cosmic dark. In our obscurity, in all this vastness, there is no hint that help will come from elsewhere to save us from ourselves.

The Earth is the only world known so far to harbor life. There is nowhere else, at least in the near future, to which our species could migrate. Visit, yes. Settle, not yet. Like it or not, for the moment the Earth is where we make our stand.

It has been said that astronomy is a humbling and character-building experience. There is perhaps no better demonstration of the folly of human conceits than this distant image of our tiny world. To me, it underscores our responsibility to deal more kindly with one another, and to preserve and cherish the pale blue dot, the only home we've ever known." - Carl Sagan, Pale Blue Dot, 1994

The Pale Blue Dot, 1990

It's difficult to look at that image, understand the profound significance of the cosmic perspective and then go on to be hateful to some other person solely for the way they look, their sexuality, the place they live, or which religion they believe. It's like being in an airplane looking down at your town as you fly by 2 miles up. Looking down, you can no longer see individual people, the cars look like ants, and houses are little squares and rectangles. It's a moving sight that changes the way you view the world you once saw. Humans easily get distracted by the petty societal bubbles we build for ourselves, so drenched in our own tiny perception, so conceited in our views of ourselves, we rarely even attempt to contemplate the world from the cosmic perspective. Humans are fearful animals, quick to hate things they do not understand, and quick to hate things that are different from their own comfortable beliefs. If we stay in our bubbles too long we become overprotective of them and tend to feel threatened by countering ideas. Just imagine how much hatred, bigotry, and homophobia would be reduced if we saw the Earth as it really is, a dot. A world in which all we have is each other, a world that is fragile, finite, and lonely, cast into a mysterious, dark, and cold corner of the universe. The religious idea that the Jews are the chosen people out of all the people of the Earth fades away as you look at that dot. The view that the Sun and all of the stars revolve around the Earth quickly dissolves. The view that there's a human-like creator of the universe who cares what one species of ape on that fraction of a dot does, says, prays about, and thinks, utterly disintegrates as you gaze at that pale blue dot. A newly established appreciation, for what we are and what we have, emerges when I look at that image. It's not just that we are small and that the universe is big, it's that we are positioned in the universe in a way that challenges what we intuitively think about our place in it. We are amazingly aware and conscious of this mysterious universe for a small while which is deeply moving to ponder about. I laugh at the petty prejudices and hateful dogma that we succumb to when we bask in our bubbles of delusion. The Pale Blue Dot is perhaps the most important photo humanity has ever captured. It's a constant reminder of our true place in the cosmos, a constant challenge to our anthropocentrism.

In 1995, Sagan became very ill with myelodysplasia, a cancer of the bone marrow, and required a blood transfusion which remarkably his sister was a perfect match for. At the time, one of his last books was published called "The Demon-Haunted World." In it, he expresses the importance of critical thinking and the role science literacy plays in society. He stressed the value of the falsification process, how we know things are true. If someone makes an unfalsifiable claim, one which cannot be tested nor debunked, how does one know they aren't lying, making it up, or simply wrong? Sagan makes a great analogy in his book illustrating the issue with the example of a dragon in a garage. Let's say I claim to have a fire-breathing dragon in my garage. You want to take a look for yourself so I open my garage and say "Here it is." You look around but see no dragon and in response ask, "Where is it?" I say "Oh, it's an invisible dragon." So you suggest putting flour on the ground to detect the dragon footprints. "Won't work," I say, "This dragon floats in the air." You suggest using an infrared sensor to detect the invisible fire. "Good idea, but the invisible fire is also heatless," I say. You'll spray-paint the dragon to make it visible. "Good idea, but the paint won't stick. This is an incorporeal dragon." As one can see here, what is the difference between an invisible, heatless, floating, incorporeal dragon and no dragon at all? If there is no way to falsify or disprove the claim of a dragon, does it really make sense to claim to know the dragon is there? Until there is evidence, some indication of the presence of the dragon, there is no reason to believe. But suppose we live in a world where millions of people claim to have these dragons in their garages. Suppose many people claim to have experiences with dragons; so we investigate further. Here is an excerpt from Sagan's book:

"Gratifyingly, some dragon-size footprints in the flour are now reported. But they're never made when a skeptic is looking. An alternative explanation presents itself. On close examination, it seems clear that the footprints could have been faked. Another dragon enthusiast shows up with a burnt finger and attributes it to a rare physical manifestation of the dragon's fiery breath. But again, other possibilities exist. We understand that there are other ways to burn fingers besides the breath of invisible dragons. Such "evidence" — no matter how important the dragon advocates consider it — is far from compelling. Once again, the only sensible approach is tentatively to reject the dragon hypothesis,

to be open to future physical data, and to wonder what the cause might be that so many apparently sane and sober people share the same strange delusion." - Carl

Sagan 1995

There is perhaps no more relevant time to note what Carl Sagan stressed here than today. Sagan died just before the internet exploded in popularity around the world, yet he foresaw the fundamental issue that plagues

us today exacerbated by the internet. We are bombarded by information daily, down to the minute. One click or scroll can lead you down a rabbit hole of fake stories, pseudoscience, misinformation, new-age spirituality, crystal healing, tarot card reading, and horoscopes. We need to be more cautious than ever to not be fooled by what people tell us. We need to remember how susceptible we are to being guided by pure emotion, believing in things that feel good to us, rather than things that are true.

Sagan also warned of a society that does not take science literacy seriously. A society that depends on science and technology in which its people don't even understand science and technology, is a society that is doomed. We are more prone to intellectual failure today than ever before because of how we've arranged social media. The most entertaining creators get rewarded with the most attention. Attention spans are decreasing as it's become easy to scroll through hundreds of quick 10-second videos that deliver cheap laughs and mindless reactions. It's seen as "cool" to not know science, those who do are dismissed as "nerds." Science education in the media is almost nonexistent and the ratio of misinformation versus actual science is at an all-time high. Here's an excerpt from what Sagan said in his book in 1995:

"I have a foreboding of an America in my children's or grandchildren's time - when the United States is a service and information economy; when nearly all the key manufacturing industries have slipped away to other countries; when awesome technological powers are in the hands of a very few, and no one representing the public interest can even grasp the issues; when the people have lost the ability to set their own agendas or knowledgeably question those in authority; when clutching our crystals and nervously consulting our horoscopes, our critical faculties in decline, unable to distinguish between what feels good and what's true, we slide, almost without noticing, back into superstition and darkness. The dumbing down of America is most evident in the slow decay of substantive content in the enormously influential media, the 30-second sound bites (now down to 10 seconds or less), lowest common denominator programming, credulous presentations on pseudoscience and superstition, but especially a kind of celebration of ignorance. As I write, the number one video cassette rental in America is the movie Dumb and Dumber. Beavis and Butthead remain popular (and influential) with young TV viewers. The plain lesson is that study and learning - not just of science, but of anything - are avoidable, even undesirable.

We've arranged a global civilization in which the most crucial elements - transportation, communications, and all other industries; agriculture, medicine, education, entertainment, protecting the environment; and even the key democratic institution of voting - profoundly depend on science and technology. We have also arranged things so that almost no one understands science and technology. This is a prescription for disaster. We might get away with it for a while, but sooner or later this combustible mixture of ignorance and power is going to blow up in our faces."

- Carl Sagan 1995

Carl Sagan

Sagan sadly died in December of 1996 at the age of 62 due to pneumonia. His influence on my life and the lives of millions around the world will always remain. His love for science was infectious and inspired many. He showed us that science is much more than just a collection of facts, it's a way of thinking that can empower us not only mentally but also emotionally. The standard view is that science is void of any excitement or emotional experience. Sagan showed us quite the opposite, that science can be the most emotionally uplifting and humbling endeavor a human can take on. People tend to look for meaning and purpose in religion or fantasy, but Sagan suggested that perhaps we are the custodians of life's meaning. Sagan's life was about a child with dreams who was able to make those dreams come true and more, by pursuing science. Sagan envisioned a world for the future in which we become a multi-planetary species, our destiny freely roaming and soaring across the cosmos; the issues of climate change, war, and chauvinism far behind us. I share this vision, which can be achieved if we shift our views on science, meaning and purpose, and our place in the universe. It is natural to ask ourselves what our significance is here in this grand universe. However, as Carl Sagan said, do something worthwhile, "If we crave some cosmic purpose, let us find ourselves a worthy goal."

PAIN, SUFFERING
AND LOSS

The moment we feel the worst as we go through pain, is the moment the realization settles in that the world continues on. The world marches on, regardless of how much pain or suffering any of us experience. We don't want to make sense of that, we want to feel as if we significantly matter to the world and that the world surely should take notice. It's uncomfortable to think nobody cares. This egotistical thought process is something that we all have as it is intrinsic to our human nature, and is what drives us to do and believe things. We have evolved to greatly care about our place within our social circle wanting to feel appreciated, after all, if one doesn't care they tend to grow estranged from their social tribe, leading them into an emotional downward spiral.

When we are going through some traumatic phase or pain in our life, our egotistical sides become magnified and seep into our logical side. We begin belligerently asking ourselves 'Why me'? Why can't others see what I'm going through? Why doesn't anyone care? It's as if life for everyone else is to be put on standby and the world owes us attention. The sensation, and hence understanding of pain, is deeply ingrained in our DNA and seen throughout our evolutionary history. People do their best to avoid or anticipate and brace for pain, whether immediate or future, and without much thought; it comes naturally to our mentality. Humans tend to want to feel happy as we enjoy it. We are susceptible to carrying this emotional baggage into our beliefs and behaviors.

The question, 'what happens when we die' is an emotionally loaded question. It typically presumes the universe must care for us, particularly when we die. There must be some special transition from life to death, after all, it's hard to imagine darkness forever; so, what really happens? We mourn the dead, but does the universe mourn for us? As far as I can see, life for us after death is the same as life for us before life; it doesn't exist. We don't experience darkness, we experience nothing as we have nothing to experience with. Death is unfathomable because all we can fathom is life. The closest one can get to understanding the notion of no experience is analogously asking one to see with their ears. What do my ears see? They don't see, they can't see because they have no medium with which to see. The question is malformed and demonstrates a lack of understanding of what experience is. As far as we know, the process of death is akin to a light bulb dimming out, the energy being lost to the outside world. Neuroscience indicates that our brains are the processors behind our experiences. Various forms of information from the outside world (light, sound, smell, touch, tastes) stream into our sensory systems, and from this information, the brain generates a map of reality, which we call "experience". All of our thoughts, feelings, and dreams are generated by the brain, as it is electrochemically stimulated by energy from the outside world. This is ultimately what pain and suffering are, the brain's chemical response to certain stimuli. And they are some of the most powerful experiences we can experience as humans. Memory is stored in the hippocampus of the brain when the most powerful neural connections are produced, which is why we tend to remember painful events. This is why it is exceedingly difficult for us to reconcile with the notion that the world is indifferent to our experiences because they are quite literally the most real things about our existence.

My grandfather died unexpectedly in late 2020, one of the first times in my life that I experienced a major loss. I remember when I received the news that night, I stepped outside and felt lost. I thought to myself as I lay on the side of my car, how could someone who meant so much to me be gone? The memories we shared together raced through my mind, the sound of his laugh, and the visual recollection of his smile illuminated inside of my head. As the notion that he was gone and that I was never going to see him again settled in, the pain worsened. I stayed out there on that chilly fall night for an hour unwilling to concede he was gone. Teary-eyed, I was pressured to make sense of my loss, even though the intriguing mystery of my grandfather's whereabouts after death still beckoned in the back of my mind. The brain's initial response to pain is to produce stress hormones like adrenaline and cortisol. The body tries to get rid of these hormones by secreting tears which contain cortisol. This is why we cry. Crying also triggers the release of opioids in the body which can better protect the immune system under stressful events. I was responding as any sane human would respond, however, my emotional brain was still combating my logical brain. How appealing was it for me to simply believe my grandfather was still with me. That he was somewhere in another realm, waiting for me to meet him again. This may seem like a strange thing to believe from any logical standpoint, and it is. But perhaps my emotional brain was tempted to believe in the afterlife because it helped counteract the pain, the rush of stress that overcame my body as I recollected my grandfather, and the impact his existence left on my brain. I quickly gathered myself, and as the adrenaline slowly subsided, I faced the fact that the world does march on. Which is okay. I remembered how fascinating it was that I was able to have an experience and share a part of my world with my grandfather for a fraction of our existence. Look at how amazing a life we had here, and the best of all it was personal and finite, something that could never be reproduced. I realized I could deal with this on my own. I didn't have to rely on the fantastical image of the afterlife to make me feel better or provide some sort of purpose or greater comfort. In fact, was I even sure the notion of an afterlife is something that was comforting in the first place? Would we be ourselves in the "afterlife," could we do things as we did in this life? Would I even want to do things there that I did here? Why even care about the afterlife? The logical inquiry of our superstitions can reveal a whole new perspective that is even more comforting than the former. A profound realization that I could become comfortable with the reality of loss.

That night, I had a vivid dream of my grandfather. I dreamt of little bits of colorful lights that swiftly assembled into my grandfather's face. The holographic image of his face that appeared gave me a warm smile. Then I hugged him and he tilted his head toward mine. I woke up soon after. It was one of the most interesting dreams I had ever had. Many people would immediately chalk that up to mean that I actually was visiting my grandfather in a spiritual realm. And how appealing would that be to believe, especially since I was grieving. Again, we have a more realistic explanation. The amygdala is the part of the brain that is more active during REM sleep. This part of the brain processes fear, anxiety and emotion. My amygdala was likely very active that night, as I was very anxious and upset. Combined with the fact that I was viewing photos and images of my grandfather just before bed, those parts of the brain most likely yielded the dream I had during REM sleep. I haven't had a powerfully vivid dream since then, just as I haven't been as emotionally stimulated since then. Evidence that my experience was most likely a product of what my brain activity was doing that night. There is no good reason to believe that dream correlated to something real at all. We must exhaust all possibilities in the order of the least substantive or least likely, to most substantive and most likely before I can remotely assert it was "god" or a "higher realm" that I experienced. Assessing the spectrum of possibilities allows one to recognize that some explanations *can not* be discounted from our conclusions, this is how science works and why it continues to work. I want to be an example of someone who, although would love to believe that they actually contacted their deceased grandfather, dignifiedly withholds that belief in virtue of lack of evidence yet remains open to new evidence and healthily skeptical. If it happens to be that one day we discover there was something real happening there, then great, I would be the first one to concede. However, the evidence just isn't there. As I've learned before, humans are susceptible to delusion and mistakes. I could be fatally wrong about my faith, or worse, I may attach myself to some wishful belief that prevents me from seeing a more powerful and beautiful fact of reality.

FOOL'S GOLD

[1]

Pyrite

Tell someone who is scientifically illiterate that they're made of star stuff and in response, they may look confused, look at you funny or maybe even laugh. They may ask malformed questions in an attempt to attack your position, but in actuality, they do nothing and are wild misinterpretations of what the opponent thinks. Your opponent must first have at least a basic understanding of star formation, nuclear fusion leading to larger elements, star death, accretion disks, and Earth's formation in order to remain relevant in that conversation. "If we come from monkeys why do monkeys still exist?" Scientifically illiterate people may often misunderstand one notion of biological evolution for example and then suffer a bad case of confirmation bias as they proclaim evolution can't be true, or worse, proclaim they believe in microevolution but not macroevolution. This is a major problem in thinking as you may see. Not only because they must be corrected that micro and macroevolution refer to the same biological process but because the rest of their thinking branches off into a muddy mess of confusion, ironically thinking they have it all figured out. The issue is a compounding one because they are basing their entire belief on a set of false assumptions. It's like you're trying to mine for gold and as you dig you stumble across fool's gold, which is the nickname for a common lustrous sulfide mineral called pyrite. Not knowing better, you excitedly assume it's real gold so you keep digging, collecting as much as you can find thinking you're going to be rich. You prematurely purchase a loan on a new car, you max out your credit cards, and you quit your job, assuming they'll all be paid off as you've struck gold! Only to bring your findings to a gold buyer who shows you that your 2 tons of rock are worthless. This is the house of cards I am warning believers from building. Believers are typically emotionally motivated to believe in their particular religion or spirituality, they carry a lot of emotional baggage with their beliefs. Many believers hold their beliefs dearly and personally, they become so attached that the ideology is assumed as part of their personality. Not only do they begin naively considering any counter ideas as threats or "disrespect" to their personhood, but they are naively carrying all of their eggs in one basket. It's as if they put on god goggles and now only see reality through the filter of their particular belief, everything becomes "god's creation," morality can only come from "god," the universe could only be configured by "god." This can have damaging consequences to those around them not only because they can be fatally wrong about what they believe, which could also be emotionally devastating for them down the road to concede to; even more detrimental, they may also feel as if they are granted the right, in virtue of their belief system, to become hateful, bigoted and homophobic towards others without even knowing it. These are toxic mental attitudes that a secular person may desperately want to warn the believer of. But as damaging as fool's gold may be, I believe sometimes all of us need to be fooled once in a while. We all should be lucky to get the chance to have our worldviews crumble before us, leaving us emotionally

and intellectually stung by superior countering viewpoints. It teaches one of the greatest lessons about open-mindedness in life that sticks with us forever. As

I mentioned in one of the earlier chapters, when I left religion it was emotionally challenging. A belief I held dearly for 20 years of my life, I saw it as part of my being. Could that pain have been suppressed if I had left religion earlier? Maybe. However, I doubt it would have left such a lasting impact on my mentality as it did when I left. Sometimes I do wish I would have left religion earlier, but the perspective it enabled me to have, the ability to put myself in the shoes of a believer, able to put on that pair of god goggles at a moment's notice, is simply invaluable. I know what it is like to believe, and I also know what it's like to be fooled, whereas the typical believer may not know what it's like to *not* believe. Perhaps there is no better lesson we could receive than to be mistaken, deeply wrong, fooled by fool's gold.

I recall going to church when I was younger, being captivated by the intricate architecture carved into the cathedral walls, the colorful stained glass projecting the angelic characters of the biblical stories, and the beautiful echoes of Christian hymns reverberating across the thinness of the air encapsulated by the large and elaborately decorated plastered walls. People attentively standing in their pews faced forward, responding to the priests' calls to recite a prayer or profess the Nicene creed, waiting to hear the sacred gospel accounts. The seriousness of the experience at church; the conviction of the congregation can give the false impression of realness. The euphoria one can feel when subjected to that type of experience can give the impression that something magical is being witnessed. The sights and sounds at church stimulate dopamine and feel-good chemicals to rush through the brain, further cementing the churchgoers association between happiness or lightness with religion. Does it seem like fool's gold to you? This type of fool's gold is no longer in rock form but in thought form. The delusion brought about by our emotional brain when overstimulated with good feelings can cause us to believe in strange things without even realizing it. As a child especially, I had no way of distinguishing between what was simply a good feeling brought about by my brain chemistry versus what was real.

Humans subconsciously communicate in several ways; hand movements, facial expressions, pauses between words or sentences, special pronunciation of certain trigger words, etc. Often people can become hypnotized by these subliminal messages when carefully displayed. Countless religious preachers, physics and mediums, and spiritual channelers I have observed will use certain keywords, keyphrases, or hand gestures, that from experience, they find resonates with listeners. They are carefully designed to hypnotize the listener into thinking the speaker is trustworthy and honest, when indeed the speaker may have great conviction in their beliefs, yet be spouting falsehoods or pseudoscience. The scientifically illiterate unskeptical listener can be easily drawn in by the poetic words and messages of any preacher that knows how to visually, emotionally, and linguistically captivate an audience.

"It's not a religion it's a relationship," you'll often hear. This is clearly a ridiculous statement as christianity and jesus's story are indeed parts of a religion. Yet apologists understand that people are generally sick of religious dogma so they leverage the emotionally charged story of jesus' death and crucifixion to captivate people. "Jesus didn't die for you so that you could sin," they'll often shout as if we are supposed to feel terrible and ashamed for existing, so we must turn to their belief system. They'll often claim that fear vanishes when one believes in god, omitting the fact that fear is what drove them to that belief in the first place. Fear and happiness, sacrifice and reward, cortisol and dopamine, are largely what drive humans. Emotional reward and satisfaction are perhaps the most enticing type of fool's gold in existence, the most difficult to resist.

Near-death experiences and out-of-body experiences can have the same effect on the human psyche. I've never experienced an NDE, however, we know they happen quite often, as millions of people have had them. In these experiences people report feeling extremely light and peaceful, claiming to have seen "heaven" or "hell". They claim to be able to see their bodies from afar as if their "soul" ascended from their bodies and are witnessing our world from a separate spiritual realm. One can find hundreds of videos and testimonies online of people going through these experiences proclaiming it is evidence of a god or spiritual guidance. Think of how convincing such an experience would be to someone who is scientifically illiterate. We know that cultural background has an impact on how people have these experiences and what they claim to have seen. We also know that it is possible to induce NDEs and OBEs in patients at will by applying an electrical charge to certain parts of the brain. One explanation is that as the heart is resuscitated back to a regular rhythm, the brain switches between different levels of consciousness, and a malfunction can occur stimulating the visual cortex and giving the patients hallucinations, similar to claims of seeing "light." Scientists can also induce out of body experiences with hallucinogens, and tests have been performed on patients to determine whether or not they can actually see beyond the operating table. One 2014 study called "Awareness during Resuscitation" involved the investigation of cardiac survivors from multiple hospitals and hundreds of interviews. Researchers placed pictures on shelves that would only be viewable from above. The study found none of the patients could accurately identify the pictures from the shelves. Of course, more research surely needs to be done. Like Sagan's dragon in the garage there very well could be some supernatural truth to these experiences. However, no such verifiable evidence to confirm this actually exists. Plus, there are more compelling naturalistic explanations available. We must withhold belief until more evidence is available. We often find it appealing to sneak the supernatural into the gaps of our understanding, driven by some false presumptions. The emotional brain when left unscathed by logical thought can lead to remarkably inaccurate conclusions. The human brain is a complex mechanism of a hundred billion neurons and synapses with multiple parts working simultaneously to produce your perspective of reality. We must consider that this mechanism is not perfect, and often makes errors. According to the World Health Organization, 6% of people in the general population have experienced at least one hallucination in their lives that was not caused by drugs, alcohol, dreaming, or mental illness. Given a world population of 8 billion, that would correspond to 480 million healthy people who have experienced a hallucination at least once in their lives, around the world. Mix this susceptibility to human error and tendency to be guided by emotion with ignorance of world facts, and the end product is a delusion. Think of how prone we are to making errors in judgment, being incorrect or severely mistaken. We must reserve extra skepticism for when we encounter an idea that sounds awfully enticing to believe in, otherwise, we may bet everything we know we have, for fool's gold.

FREE WILL

The classical Newtonian view of physics defies what we typically refer to when we conceptualize "free will". Frequently discussed in philosophical or religious discussions is the topic of free will because it has massive implications for particular worldviews. "Free will" generally means the ability to freely choose an action without any external intervention. I think what we are referring to when we invoke the notion of free will is essentially meaningless. Under the classical view of physics, every action you take has a prior cause. So if I'm presented with an apple or an orange, and I decide to take the apple, that may seem as if it was a free action. However, something prior had caused me to choose the apple. We now know in neuroscience that the brain is generally what produces thoughts and sends signals throughout your body to initiate the actions you take. This would follow that our brains are what determine our actions. The consensus in neuroscience is fairly clear, many of them using this argument as a defeater to free will under the aforementioned definition. Scientists can use fMRI to measure the spike in brain activity *ten seconds* before there's even an intention for the subject to make a choice. The brain clearly has a massively fundamental influence on our actions. There are documented cases of people who have developed brain tumors in which their personality and even their behavior dramatically change in comparison before the tumor and after the tumor is surgically removed. Stunningly, a large majority of prisoners across the world have brain injuries, as multiple studies have shown. Operating under the classical laws of physics, we are evidently completely subject to what our brains are doing. But the big question here is, *who* controls the brain? Am I the one controlling my brain right now as I type these words? Wouldn't I be considered my brain though? What does "me" truly mean? Is the self a real thing or conceptual? These are profound questions. It seems to me that if the brain is a physical entity along with our thoughts which are electrical impulses produced by the brain, then all of the above must abide by the same laws of physics. If every one of our thoughts is determined by the laws of physics, which seems to be the case, then the free will advocates have no argument left. The laws of physics determined every thought, determined every letter I am typing at this very moment, determined every cause and effect which ultimately means we can't have free will. If all we are is essentially collections of molecules temporarily arranged in this configuration due to the laws of physics operating on each one of our atoms, then there can also be no real sense of the self. We can longer see "ourselves" as somehow separate from nature and its laws, which is what we do when we typically mean the self, but we must see ourselves as part of the universe going through the motions. When we say 'I chose to go to movies', technically I should be saying the laws of nature determined that the collection of particles that call itself "I" go to the movies. The self seems to be a powerful persistent illusion brought up by the brain. Every roughly 40 days, most of your skin cells die and are replaced, which means your skin is an entirely new set of matter. In fact, every 7 years roughly, nearly all of your body's cells die and are replaced by new cells, with the exception of most neurons which is why you retain memory for a lifetime. But the rest of your body essentially is constantly being replaced over your lifetime. In this view, the self is an illusion, and what we refer to as the self is really just borrowed matter that temporarily gives you the sense of being an individual free agent.

Now there are some that argue free will can lie within the indeterministic or random nature of quantum mechanics, where particles can exist in a state of superposition sharing multiple states at once, unable to determine where the particle will be at any given location, only able to determine the probability of finding the particle in the given location. However, we can still argue that there may be some deterministic factor controlling the behavior of particles on the quantum level that we have yet to identify. The compatibilist may argue that although we can't control the external forces that determine us to do things, we can still control the internal forces, to which I would clearly disagree since there would be no distinction between internal and external forces, just the same set of laws of nature. Nevertheless, I am open to any notion of free will or compatibilism if quantum mechanics points to it, however, I am not aware of any such convincing views.

What are the implications of determinism for a secular person? There are none! My life doesn't change simply for recognizing or holding to determinism. I clearly do not act as if I am determined, for all intents and purposes I act as if I have free will. In fact, it would be difficult for me to act as if I did not have free will, that is how potent the illusion of free will is to us. Our brains just simply can not deal with that counter-intuitiveness, we did not evolve to think with modern physics in mind. Whether or not free will exists is completely irrelevant to me as we can live our lives just fine acting as if we are free, yet technically recognizing determinism is true under further scrutiny. But to a person of Abrahamic faith, the lack of free will can quite literally be the most damaging notion for their worldview. The idea that there is an ultimate authority judging every one of our actions absolutely depends on free will being true. Otherwise, it wouldn't make sense for a god to judge us if we have no control over our actions. Determinism is perhaps the best argument against the standard Abrahamic faiths. But in defense of some of the critiques the secular hard determinists may receive from religious viewpoints, namely the meaning of prison if we have no control over our actions, allow me to explain. At first glance this seems like a good refutation, why care about someone's actions or put them in jail if they didn't control anything about that crime they committed? The short answer is that humans prefer to foster a society in which less crime is committed. So regardless if you chose the action or not, society will still be determined to want to imprison the criminal by virtue of preference. For example, if I build a robot equipped with guns and ammo that I programmed to kill with, it will inevitably kill since it was determined to do so. Yet no rational person would allow the robot to continue killing people with the defense that the robot was determined to do so. Of course not! Any sane person would call for that robot to be taken out of society or destroyed. The same applies to the prison system. To touch on the idea that determinism strips us of any meaning, love, or creativity, I will say I disagree. As physicist Brian Greene elegantly put it, even though our actions may be determined, we are the most immediate cause of our actions, they emerge through us, through our particles, such that when hit with certain stimuli causes us to do those things. Love is still equally real in a deterministic world since we are the most immediate particles that are collectively experiencing this emergent property of love.

THE ORIGINS OF RELIGION AND ITS PLACE

For as long as we remain human, religion will have a place in our world. Abrahamic religions are indeed dying across the western world at record rates, and I attribute that to the internet enabling the widespread exposure of the toxicity of those religions. However, new religions, potentially global religions, will emerge. Humans love to adhere to the beliefs that appease their fantasies, and religion is a way of satisfying that urge to want to explain the mysteries of the world yet be comfortable within that finely tuned paradigm. Notions of good and evil are also common themes in religion because morality is so natural and obvious to humans. We have a clear sense of the experiences which we feel are bad like droughts, floods, disease, death, and experiences we feel are good such as love, sacrifice, control, and peace. It's clear these themes which have been innately tied to our being throughout our evolution, are going to show up in religion. Even some animals such as several species of monkeys, apes, dolphins, and elephants show clear signs of performing basic religious rituals. African elephants perform funeral rituals; they not only grieve after the deaths of fellow members but they have also been shown to help other elephants in need. Morality is an emergent property of mammalian brains. Just as our brains have evolved, so have religions. The emergence of polytheistic religions has roots in agriculture, as the ancients settled and were able to comprehend large-scale cultivation and harvesting of food, they felt a sense of control over their environment. This sense of control was imposed upon the natural world, leading people to believe events like thunder, or rain were also controlled by some higher agencies. These gods were the accumulated result of the personification of the universe. Out of selfishness, ancient people would promise devotion to their imagined higher powers in exchange for a good harvest or a good hunt. Just as we promise devotion to others, in exchange for approval or gifts from others. Humans have always thought that in order for good to happen, they needed to give something to receive something in return. The sacrificing of animals by humans was very common in ancient societies, as they thought animals had souls or were given to us by the gods. As you can see, the theme of sacrifice and karma, especially sacrifice in exchange for a reward, carried into the monotheistic religions. The ancient Babylonians followed the monotheistic Zoroastrian religion nearly 4000 years ago. They worshiped one god called Ahura Mazda, they believed that he created the world, and that good deeds would enable one to get to heaven. Zoroastrians prayed five times a day according to their holy scripture, The Avesta. According to their afterlife as written in the

Avesta, people get weighed on a scale; if their sins outweigh their good deeds, they would get sent to the fires of hell and vice versa. It was the official religion in several areas of Persia until the 7th century AD when the Muslims invaded.

The origin of Judaism, Christianity, and Islam starts with the ancient Hebrews believing in one god, Yahweh, who chose to make a covenant with Abraham, granting him rewards if he followed certain rules from god. As the years went by and Abraham's descendants fell through with following god's laws, several prophets were supposedly sent down to Earth by god in order to get people back on track to righteousness. One popular preacher named Jesus, would preach righteousness and be outspoken against the rich; he was radical and anti-authoritarian, and seen as a threat to the Roman government. Many people who lived in poverty regarded Jesus as their savior, and consequently, rumors spread that he performed miracles and healed people's illnesses. For centuries, the Jews believed in a Messiah who would come to establish a new everlasting kingdom. Since the Roman empire was in decline at the time, the Jews found it easy to believe that Jesus was the Messiah. Centuries after Jesus was killed by the Romans, many people still believed that Jesus would one day come back to save them. Roman emperor Constantine in the 4th century AD, in an effort to unite the Roman empire, succumbed to the people and instilled Christianity as the empire's religion. This allowed the spread of Christianity from that time until the present day.

The story of Jesus is not totally unique. Throughout history, there have been several prophets who have been claimed to resurrect and perform miracles, be the sons of gods, and even be born of virgins. People willing to die and sacrifice their lives for these prophets or gods were not uncommon. Even within the bible, the concept of resurrection is not unique to jesus, as in Matthew 27:52 the bible states that many tombs broke open and saints were raised for the dead, appearing to people in Jerusalem. People saw tremendous hope in these myths, especially people in ancient times when life was dramatically more difficult than it is today. This is mainly why these myths are seamlessly passed down, with additional claims and rumors sprinkled into the stories as they are orally spread. It's analogous to the game "telephone," where one original message is to be passed down to a line of people, and by the time the message is announced by the last person, it is wildly different or exaggerated from the original message. As you can likely get the point here, it is no surprise why humans seriously engage with religious beliefs, people tend to use religion as a mental escape or to get away from the real world. Even though I am against the violence, hatred, and bigotry some of these myths can perpetuate, I am not against the exercise of religion itself, as it still has its place in society.

Today in the western world, Marvel comics can be seen as a religion. People gather from all across the world religiously to watch the Marvel movies starring their favorite superheroes. For those two and half hours in the theaters, the audience pretends as if their beloved superheroes really exist, emotionally invested in the storyline and origins of each character, wishing that they could be a part of their world or share some of their powers. We love our Spiderman backpacks, clothing with Iron-man printed on it proudly demonstrating our love and allegiance to these characters. Comic-Con can be seen as an annual ritual or religious tradition, where all followers gather and dress up in their character's signature costumes and recite their character's sayings and behaviors. What really is the difference between Marvel of today and the ancient mythology of the past? Well, we know better today how to distinguish mythological realms from reality. We don't like to admit it, but we concede these Marvel characters don't really exist, unlike the ancient people who may have otherwise really been convinced. When we leave the theaters or when we leave Comic-Con, we set aside those mythologies and move on with reality. Still, part of our nature wants to feel like we belong to something greater; and this feeling is something to celebrate! We should be deeply ecstatic to have the ability to use our imagination, bringing us to possible worlds, or even worlds that can never physically exist. It stirs up our creativity, it bubbles our curiosity; imagination is a powerful tool we must utilize and cherish as long as we're human. However, we must also be responsible enough to be able to distinguish what is imaginary from what is reality.

If I have children, I will present to them a wide range of various religious and spiritual literature throughout their upbringing. I will share with them all of the teachings and laws of the bible, I will teach them the surahs of the quran, and I will educate them on Greek mythology, the karmic faiths of hinduism and buddhism. I will, without filter or bias, make sure they are religiously literate, and thoroughly understand the themes and beliefs accumulated by great religious thinkers of the past. However, I will also, without a filter, present to them the scientific method, the works, and legacies of Pythagoras, Galileo, Kepler, Newton, Faraday, Maxwell, Darwin, Einstein, and Hawking. I will ensure that my children are also scientifically literate such that they understand the consequences and the powerful fruits of science, offering them the world through a cosmic perspective. I will let them decide, in their own timing, which pathway toward the truth to choose. It will be utterly irrelevant to me which one they pick. I will refuse to force my children to put on god goggles at their conception. But you're damn right if you think that after being given all of the unbiased information, they will hesitate before picking ancient mythology as a pathway to the truth!

WHY I CARE

As I write this, the first successful nuclear fusion experiments have been performed illuminating the future potential of unlimited energy generation for our civilization. We are broadening space exploration with NASA's Artemis mission to the Moon with eyes on Mars, the James Webb Space Telescope has successfully been sent out into space capturing never before seen images of our cosmos peering deeper into our origins. Breakthroughs in artificial intelligence are enabling exponential growth in technological advancements on all fronts, which have the capacity to change our species forever. These deeply encouraging leaps in our capabilities utterly shake our world, they reinvigorate us and get us falling in love with humanity and our accomplishments once again. From my perspective, I can't help but imagine a world where we set aside our petty hatred towards one another and focus on the bigger picture for the future of humanity. Every scientific discovery we make is a reminder that we are capable of greatness. A scientifically literate person sees the world much differently than the average person; rather than seeing a bleak world filled with problems, they see a world littered with potential solutions, in every circumstance; they see a world that could be. With all of the chaos in the world, science and technology are relentlessly unleashing glimpses of a more abundant and prosperous humanity. We are deeply thrilled and excited when scientific breakthroughs and discoveries are made, they reach the largest media outlets and are broadcasted all around the world because we know that science is here to benefit all people, no matter their race, gender, or social status. Science is a beacon of hope for all of us, continually illuminating a reality once made of dreams. From the electricity that powers our homes and buildings, the medicine and vaccines invented to keep us alive and well, to the transistors in your phone or the computer which allowed you to read this very sentence, things our ancestors just a few hundred years ago would have seen as wizardry; we've made extraordinary scientific progress since the dawn of the industrial revolution and it's been because many have dared to become students of the universe. For centuries, science has been the engine of progress and prosperity, and there is much more progress to be made.

However, as our knowledge and power increase, so do the problems that come with them. Climate change, nuclear war, and economic inequality are some of the growing pains of a global civilization exiting its adolescence. The increasing complexity of our technology and utilization of energy yields a corresponding increase in the complexity of the issues that follow. Yet, we remain human, with all of the primitive traits we've carried over throughout our biological evolution. Greed, ignorance, fear, and delusion still have the capacity to wreak havoc on our civilization, destroying us within a generation. This generation is one of the most crucial moments in human history, a time when we live in a society that depends on science and technology, yet few understand how they work. Accustomed to the comforts and quality of life which we naively forget science and technology have provided for us, we have become complacent in our lack of scientific inquiry, driven by feel-good entertainment instead, gradually losing interest in any of the intellectual awareness required to solve or prevent the issues that could lead to our demise. Worse, it has become easy for billions of people to scroll on social media and get lost in cheap entertaining content or worse yet, pseudoscience and conspiracy theories. Misinformation is more accessible and inadvertently thrown in our faces than ever before, it's important that people are equipped with bullshit detectors. Think of how influential a single person can be on social media today, people are extremely susceptible to being misinformed and tricked by their favorite influencers. People can search for these influencers at will, holding to anyone they like as reliable sources; engorging themselves with endless pseudoscience and public comments that confidently agree, providing further fuel for their confirmation bias.

Those same people can vote. The stakes are higher than ever as each one of our votes cast for the leaders of our choices can impact the trajectory of our society. I remember in 2014, Republican leader Inhofe presented a snowball on the Senate floor in an attempt to refute climate change as if one snowfall debunks climate change. Thankfully Senator Whitehouse was there to correct him, but if the general population continues voting science deniers into Congress, eventually there will be no Congress for us to deny science in. Donald Trump's presidency set back scientific progress by perhaps decades. Trump's administration took the US out of the Paris climate agreement, abolished the Environmental Protection Agency, neglected climate change by rolling back emissions regulations, called a deadly pandemic a "hoax" delaying action that likely killed thousands, and tried to call for us to rake leaves to fight global warming-induced wildfires. Fostering a society that is prone to voting or acting in a detrimental way to the rest of us by virtue of their lack of scientific understanding, is one of the largest problems I can think of. It's like a rupture in a sewage line that is about to burst open. The solution stems from scientific literacy, which all people should have a basic understanding of. Now, don't think I'm calling for everyone to drop what they are doing to become a scientist. You do not have to be a scientist in order to become scientifically literate. What I am calling for is for people to magnify their curiosity, ask more questions, understand the scientific method, be open to others' ideas, understand what evidence and falsification mean, and indeed, learn more about the world around them. The future of our society depends on it. If we as a people cannot even understand the issues facing our society, how are we going to solve the issues? What are the consequences of a society that has great power but no responsibility, and no care for knowledge? Only about half of Americans agree that climate change is human-caused. That is 160 million people in the largest economy of the world that do not agree with basic science; this number is frankly embarrassing. How can we solve these global issues when half of us are even unaware of what's happening? There is enough misinformation online to give some people the illusion that there are good arguments to be heard from the other side but that is not the case at all. Climatic changes are virtually unseen on a day-to-day basis, it takes decades for the damage to actualize but it is not linear, it is exponential in severity. We can not think linearly about these issues. Hence we must foster a society that can think critically, as well as on an additive basis, one that is able to grasp the long-term complexities of the issues at hand.

Why do I attack religion or the notion of god? Why do I ask people for evidence of god and start conversations or engage in debate? Firstly, if you think my goal is to make everyone an atheist, you have it wrong. Not only would that be impossible to do, but most importantly my goal is much deeper than that. We've fostered a society in which it has become taboo to talk about religion or god, and people have grown fearful of being outspoken about these foundational beliefs. And that is precisely the big problem in my view. Society treats these beliefs as sacred, so people treat them as such. We cowardly hide in these religious bubbles, close our ears and bask in our own delusions, becoming so attached to these beliefs that we treat them as part of our personality. This tradition is passed down to our children where they learn the same behavior, and this continues generation after generation until we create a world in which secularists or anyone who tries to combat their sacred ideologies is seen as invaders. Worse, believers may hold views that are detrimental to human rights, LGBT rights, bodily rights, etc., and not even know the harm they are causing others when mindlessly voting with these ideologies in mind. Our beliefs do not exist in a vacuum in modern society, beliefs can influence how we vote, act and behave, consequently affecting others. I often get asked to not disrespect religion, yet how is it possible to disrespect a non-sentient entity and do harm? Believers aren't beliefs, they are people; criticizing religion is not practicing disrespect to any person, it is the practice of free speech. Believers commonly fall victim to emotional attachment towards one belief, and like a roadblock, it prevents them from getting past it. No belief nor idea should be exempt from criticism simply because a believer has an emotional attachment to it.

Yet we live in an upside-down world where religious criticism is seen as monstrous. For this reason, hard questions are not asked enough in our social environment. Even for the first 20 years of my life, I had never encountered a single person who asked me difficult questions about my beliefs or even expressed true opposition towards me. This is the underlying issue that I see, and my approach is to get right to the hard questions. Be upfront, direct and loud. Show opposition, show that there even is opposition in the first place as many of us are not exposed to. Once I strike a weak spot in the foundation of a belief system, the rest of it can fall easier. One question may be all it takes to shake that one belief and eventually have the rest tumble to the ground. It's like the chains to an anchor holding a ship from sailing away. One shattered belief may break the chain attached to the last anchor that was preventing someone from sailing free, looking at the world in a totally different, freeing, and open way. It also may be the first puff of smoke that alarms someone to pursue scientific inquiry and investigation. Conversations and debates may even help free thinkers and secularists remember the importance of discussion about these big ideas, shining light on arguments or pathways to the truth they had never encountered before. Everyone is at a different stage in their journey. My goal is to challenge your thinking, and influence people to become better equipped to have more fulfilled lives.

PURPOSE AND MEANING

I often get told that 'without god, there can not be any purpose to life'. People want to know where atheists and secular people find their sense of tranquility within the chaos. This is one of the deepest, most troubling thoughts a human can contemplate. Is there a purpose for our existence? Is there a hidden reason for all of this? What keeps us moving forward? We all suspect there is something more out there, and these suspicions are not uncalled for. The universe is largely mysterious and we have no way of knowing precisely just how limited our perceptions are relative to the absolute truth if it exists. However, I can tell you that as a secular person, one without god or religious ideology, I can still thrive spiritually. And when I use the term spiritually here I am not referring to any "supernatural" sense of the word. In fact, I have a deeper, keener sense of purpose and meaning than I've ever had as a believer, and I don't know of any religion or spiritual ideology that could come close to where I source mine.

From my perspective, it is sad to hear that people feel they must cling to a god or religion to achieve comfort or purpose; god is a spiritual dead end to me. Think about it, what purpose would a "god" really give us?

Under this worldview, we are merely something god made when it was bored. It existed for an eternity and then decided to easily poof us into existence with a clap of its hands. People like to compare "god's creation" of the human body with the creation of an art piece, suggesting the intentional design of our complex physiology demonstrates its value. Where the comparison fails is that what makes an art piece valuable is not the sheer complexity of that piece, but the recognition of the fallibility and humility of the painter, and the irreplicability of the story behind the painting.

What makes Picasso's or Davinci's work amazing, what leaves us in awe as we stumble across their work, is that these painters are just people as all of us are, with access to the same tools we all have access to, yet able to express an emotionally enriched story and message behind it. So if god made us, of course it would, god can do anything; no surprise there, no hardship nor emotional baggage. In fact, god could have made a much more exciting and exquisite world than this one. To me, that worldview leaves us humans with little value to show for.

Whereas, if we *are* these collections of atoms and molecules that naturally exist without any agency guiding the laws of our nature such that when configured in specific ways, against the odds, temporarily chemically assemble into breathing, thinking humans with all the capabilities and fallibilities we have; that is something remarkably profound, utterly mind-blowing! Each one of your atoms carries the legacy of at least 13.7 billion years of natural physical evolution within the universe. If we played the universe back like a movie, we would be able to trace each one of the atoms that make up our bodies to the air and water of the Earth, to the plants and soil, and further back, spinning around the accretion disk during the early ages of the solar system, further back, in the cores of exploding stars across the galaxy, further back at the Big Bang! Every breath of air you take in contains atoms that once existed in every human being who has ever lived. Mathematically speaking, some of the atoms you have just breathed in from the air were once breathed in by Aristotle, Isaac Newton, or George Washington. This is profoundly remarkable to think about! Similarly, the complexity of our brains is amazing *because* of the fact they evolved naturally and were not designed. The capacity of the brain to have and share the thoughts, memories, dreams, and the love it produces given that it is merely a product of vast sequences of chemical processes stemming back to the Big Bang, is something that makes me fall in love with nature, as it truly exists. Evolution itself is deeply fascinating to learn about, the fact that each one of us is connected biologically to a chimpanzee-like ancestor in north central Africa 6 million years ago; we are all close family, and we're also family to every species of life on the planet. The implications of our natural human origins directly conflict with any notions of racism. How could racism even cross the mind of a scientifically literate person who understands that all humans are closely related to one another, let alone that race is a social construct? It just doesn't make sense! It's no longer 'we are the chosen people' but that *none* of us are 'chosen people'. I often get told that if love is merely chemicals then it takes meaning away from the experience. However, I suggest that the fact love *is* merely a chemical response in the brain that only makes the experience more remarkable. Look at what these basic natural chemicals can do when arranged in certain ways! It's a total 180-degree difference in thinking. How humbling of a perspective, how deeply moving of a reality to recognize. As I have learned how the world works, I have developed a deep sense of appreciation for what we are, immense value radiates from the world around me through my perspective. This spiritual fulfillment and purpose which is enabled by the scientific perspective of reality, has infiltrated almost every facet of my life and goes deeper than any religion or ideology has for me. It's one of the things that drives me to learn more about the world, it's what gives me hope for humanity and keeps me moving forward; that I can live another day, and learn something that transcends any of my life's petty problems. If I am ever going through trouble in my life, I remember this cosmic perspective, and it gets me back on track.

What about objective purpose, what is the reason for our existence itself? We tend to look outwards for meaning and purpose, we like to think there must be a purpose that transcends any of our opinions or perspectives. I ask, why *must* there be some intrinsic purpose to our existence? We find ourselves imposing our inner thinking onto the world around us out of fear or discomfort. It is uncomfortable to concede the bad things that occur in our lives do not have a higher reason behind them, conversely, it's hard to fall in love with someone and not think it was meant to be. It is appealing for many to simply conclude "god" gives us purpose and leave it at that. 'If you would just read this holy book here, you'll see the purpose that god revealed to us.' However, that would mean our purpose is *told* to us as if we must simply accept it even though we may want other things for our lives. Imagine a father telling his child that he or she was born to be a lawyer. If his child wants to be an astronaut, does that mean the child no longer has a purpose nor can find meaning in life? This is the type of conundrum that can follow if you believe we are given a specific purpose. If I asked a believer what their purpose was according to their god, they would likely say something like 'our purpose is to have a relationship with the creator and praise him.' Is *that* our only purpose; the only reason we exist is to emotionally stimulate a lonely being who is repeatedly called "perfect"? And how obvious an anthropogenic purpose is that? It seems to me that humans would be the ones who think relationships are purposeful. Maybe we are personifying god again, imposing our human perspective on the concept. Maybe everything I've said comes back to the fact that purpose is purely subjective. We can generate meaning and purpose, it emerges through the interactions we have with one another. I can discover an infinite amount of purpose and meaning in the world around me once I detach myself from the idea that "god" is the sole authority, the only one who could give it to us. We don't need a god to give us or tell us our purpose, we can make it ourselves, and we can find it on our own.

As soon as this idea clicked for me, it only emphasized the importance of my purposes. It's no longer that I must wait for my purpose to be given to me, but now I can be the custodian of life's purpose. I could get over the discomfort of there not being an objective purpose yet remain optimistic about the life we know we have and want. Optimistic nihilism is a freeing mindset to have. With this chapter, I wanted to debunk the stereotype that all atheists or secularists live without purpose, or that they have a pessimistic attitude. It may be true that each of us has a different approach to these questions and that we will perhaps never know the true answer if there is an answer. However, learning to embrace the mystery, withholding from imposing our presuppositions upon it, seems to me to be the healthiest, most productive way to move forward. In fact, succumbing to the mystery of life only fuels my desire to learn more as without mystery there is no discovery. As the great physicist Richard Feynman has said:

"I think it's much more interesting to live not knowing than to have answers which might be wrong. I have approximate answers, and possible beliefs, and different degrees of uncertainty about different things, but I am not absolutely sure of anything. There are many things I don't know anything about, such as whether it means anything to ask "Why are we here?" I might think about it a little bit, and if I can't figure it out then I go on to something else. But I don't have to know the answer. I don't feel frightened by not knowing things, by being lost in the mysterious universe without having any purpose - which is the way it really is, as far as I can tell."

— Richard P. Feynman

Where do we go from here? All we know is that no matter how unbearable the discomfort may become when questioning our existence; all we have is each other. I've concluded in my life that it's not worth it to ponder so much about this unanswerable question, instead, I focus on being the best I can be, as I see it. I want to explore the world, learn about the cosmos, build relationships with others, help as many people as I can, and leave a mark on this planet before I am gone. I wake up every day in appreciation for life and awareness itself with the recognition of what we really seem to be and what we can do within our finite time as humans. We will likely never be in this position, this moment here, ever again. Regardless of whether we turn to fertilizer after we die or we ascend to the "afterlife", *this* life, the one we are living now, is forever finite and engraved in the stones of existence. I've grown comfortable with the hidden mysteries of reality, while remaining eager to absorb as much information as I can, accepting the truth no matter where it may be. My mindset is fluid, I do not hold onto any particular ideology or worldview dearly or personally; I flow toward the evidence, not towards the ego. I can find spiritual fulfillment and be moved by reality as it *actually* exists, without having to impose my childish fantasies upon it. I can more clearly envision the world I want to see and move towards doing something that may lead to the progression of humanity as a whole. I often think of what we can accomplish as I look back at history.

I've noticed throughout history that the people who've changed the world had one thing in common; an obsession. Albert Einstein was obsessed with math and physics, he dreamed of producing a simple equation that could elegantly describe the workings of the universe; consequently, he completed the general theory of relativity forever changing physics. Carl Sagan was obsessed with going to Mars since he was a child, he dreamed of what it would be like to explore the red planet, soaring through the cosmos; consequently, he became a world-renowned astronomer forever changing how people connected to science. Stephen Hawking was obsessed with black holes, he dreamed of unveiling their hidden secrets; consequently, he discovered Hawking radiation and Area theorem, forever changing the field of astrophysics. Steve Jobs was obsessed with computers, he dreamed of changing the way people used computers; consequently, he ended up producing the iPhone forever changing technology. James Cameron was obsessed with film, he dreamed of turning the perfect scenes and characters within his imagination into reality; consequently, he produced some of the highest-grossing films of all time. All of the people above had humble or even rough beginnings, yet were led by their inner passions and obsessions to push humanity forward just a bit further while they had a chance. We stand on the shoulders of giants. I'm obsessed with learning how the world works, questioning the norm, and helping others gain new perspectives of reality. Equipped with a scientific perspective of reality, we are led down a path that enables us to achieve nearly anything if we honestly care about the truth and if we care about our future.

When I was a child, I wanted to be a magician. I loved performing magic tricks and playing pranks on people, eagerly awaiting their reactions. I would dress up in black, wave a magic wand, and perform card tricks and coin tricks, excitedly wanting to share these intriguing acts with my family and friends. Until recently, I couldn't quite describe the reason why I loved magic or messing with people as a child. I realize now it was because of the expression of surprise and astonishment that would light up people's faces as they contemplated what had just occurred in front of their eyes. In these moments, the door to a new realm of possibilities opens up, giving us a heightened sense of wonder about the world that didn't exist before. It is the same magical sensation as the childhood moment I had when I put on those eyeglasses for the first time, unveiling a world I had never seen. It is a magical experience, and I've always wanted to share these life-changing moments with others. The child version of me who created science presentations about the earth, the stars, planets, or aliens to show them to his family and friends, was me attempting to express the feeling of wonder I had felt when learning those profound ideas. This passion still lives inside of me today, and I still want to share that magic with the world, a world that seems to lack this optimism. I realize now that this is what science is doing, it continually leaves us in utter shock about a reality we would have never previously expected. The best part is that science is real, it is *really* how the world works. Discovering the universe from the smallest scales of the quantum world and living cells to the largest scales of the stars, galaxy formation, and cosmic inflation, is something magical and I could only wish everyone had the opportunity to experience it in their lifetimes. This deeper cosmic understanding transcends and utterly dwarfs any of the petty prejudices, hatreds, or egotistical notions we fall victim to in our daily lives. Science offers the greatest rewards for those of us who are daring enough to poke the universe and observe what happens, without letting what we previously believed get in the way. I know of no other human endeavor that is able to better transform the world, enrich the quality of our lives, be a relentless source of hope and inspiration for all of humanity, and be a source of astonishing wonder that deeply moves us in ways we could have never envisioned before, than acquiring the scientific perspective of life.

"Don't sit this one out. Do something. You are by accident of fate alive at an absolutely critical moment in the history of our planet."

— Carl Sagan

I've always wondered why when I find myself in nature, I feel a sense of peace, serenity, and comfort. Clearly, there is an evolutionary explanation here. I sense the green colors of the trees, the scent of the leaves and fresh air, the sound of the blissful wind, singing animals, and the warmth of the sun rays beaming down upon my skin; my brain is stimulated to release the feel-good chemicals such as oxytocin and dopamine which bring upon the sensation of happiness. And for all intents and purposes that is a good enough explanation. However, I think there's something else happening there. There's a particularly noticeable contrast between the feeling that emerges when outdoors basking in nature, compared to doing most other things, especially talking to people, even the people you love. Nature doesn't judge. Nature isn't clouded by all of the thoughts that people have. All of the bigoted thoughts, all of the resistance that builds up in our minds as we encounter collisions of worldviews and ideologies. No, nature just is. It does not care what we believe, it does not care what we believe about it and it does not have a belief about us at all. How obvious to us that nature doesn't talk, nature does not think. Perhaps there is a much deeper lesson to be learned from nature in this regard. Sometimes it can be advantageous to revisit square one with our belief systems and start from scratch. All of the toxic human judgments and preconceived notions that have built up and been carried for years in our minds about how things are *supposed* to be need to be allowed to subside once in while. Even though nature doesn't talk or think, it can surely teach us a bunch.

Printed in Great Britain
by Amazon

28268044R00071